Praise for Dean Jobb's books

Empire of Deception

Intoxicating and impressively researched, Jobb's immorality tale provides a sobering post-Madoff reminder that those who think everything is theirs for the taking are destined to be taken.

— The New York Times Book Review

Comprehensively researched and enthralling ... high-stakes drama of the first order ... unmasking [a] master swindler and revealing the author as an equally masterful storyteller.

— The Washington Post

Fans of Erik Larson will love Jobb's latest true crime masterpiece.

— Library Journal (starred review of audiobook edition)

Calculated Risk: Greed, Politics and the Westray Tragedy

A stunning book that proves that Jobb can dig as well as any Pictou County miner ... a powerful indictment of expediency taken to a senselessly tragic conclusion.

– The Globe and Mail Report on Business Magazine

I couldn't put the book down, mainly because of Jobb's ability to portray the people in the tragedy.

– Financial Times of Canada

An excellent book ... This is investigative journalism as it should be: meticulously researched, judiciously reported, and enthrallingly written.

– Canadian Book Review Annual

With painstaking diligence, Jobb pieced together a complex story ... a tale of lax safety, wrenching heartbreak and a project driven to disaster by politics and greed.

– Canadian Press

The Acadians: A People's Story of Exile and Triumph

Marries a historian's fidelity to research and detail with a journalist's ability to tell a story with verve, colour and attention to the human elements beneath the historical record. Popular history just doesn't get much better than this.

–Winnipeg Free Press

Highly authoritative ... engaging, well-written and evocative ... vivid descriptions bring people and places to life.

– Canada's History magazine

Daring, Devious and Deadly

True Tales of Crime and Justice from Nova Scotia's Past

Dean Jobb

Pottersfield Press
Lawrencetown Beach, Nova Scotia, Canada

Library and Archives Canada Cataloguing in Publication

Title: Daring, devious & deadly : true tales of crime and justice from Nova Scotia's past / Dean Jobb.
Other titles: Daring, devious and deadly | True tales of crime and justice from Nova Scotia's past
Names: Jobb, Dean, 1958- author.
Identifiers: Canadiana (print) 2020027807X | Canadiana (ebook) 20200278177 | ISBN 9781989725238 (softcover) | ISBN 9781989725245 (EPUB)
Subjects: LCSH: Crime—Nova Scotia—History. | LCSH: Criminals—Nova Scotia—History. | LCSH: Criminal justice, Administration of—Nova Scotia—History.
Classification: LCC HV6809.N6 J63 2020 | DDC 364.9716—dc23

Cover design: Gail LeBlanc

Pottersfield Press gratefully acknowledges the financial support of the Government of Canada for our publishing activities. We also acknowledge the support of the Canada Council for the Arts and the Province of Nova Scotia which has assisted us to develop and promote our creative industries for the benefit of all Nova Scotians.

Pottersfield Press
248 Leslie Road
East Lawrencetown, Nova Scotia, Canada, B2Z 1T4
Website: www.PottersfieldPress.com
To order, phone 1-800-NIMBUS9 (1-800-646-2879) www.nimbus.ns.ca

Printed in Canada

Pottersfield Press is committed to protecting our natural environment. As part of our efforts, this book is made of material from well-managed FSC®-certified forests and other controlled sources.

Contents

He may well have been the wittiest, most sarcastic judge ever to grace the bench in Canada. Magistrate A.B. MacGillivray's one-liners at the expense of offenders and lawyers who appeared in his Glace Bay courtroom became legendary. But was this any way to dispense justice?

An incendiary letter published in The Novascotian, accusing Halifax's civic leaders of corruption, landed pioneering newspaper publisher Joseph Howe in the prisoner's dock in 1835 on a charge of criminal libel. If convicted, he faced imprisonment and financial ruin. Luckily, he had a good lawyer.

When the body of the crewman of a British warship was found on the steps of a notorious Halifax tavern in 1853, there was no shortage of conflicting stories, theories, and suspects. The trial that followed would prove to be even more chaotic.

By 1870 James Forman had been the Bank of Nova Scotia's head cashier and most trusted employee for almost four decades. Too bad he was using his accounting skills to line his own pockets.

When P.T. Barnum's famous circus arrived in Halifax for the first time in the summer of 1876, a couple of enterprising bank robbers stole the show.

Introduction

"If there is one thing more than another of which the average man likes to read the details, that thing is a first-class murder with the goriest of trimmings."

– Chicago Daily Tribune,
November 17, 1880

Almost a century and a half after the *Chicago Daily Tribune* marvelled at the popularity of crime news, the appetite for accounts of the real-life exploits of criminals may be more insatiable than ever. We're in the midst of a true crime renaissance – an explosion of books, feature articles, podcasts, social media sites, television series, and movies.

True crime stories offer all the elements of the most gripping fiction – shocking acts, desperate manhunts, mysteries to be solved. And the high-stakes courtroom battles that follow, as Canada's renowned popular historian Charlotte Gray has noted, "are inherently dramatic: the imposing rituals, the cunning legal strategies, the clash of competing narratives, the unpredictability of juries." Society's ability to combat crime and punish offenders is put to the test, with the justice system itself on trial. Will justice be done? Will the guilty go free? Will the innocent be wrongly convicted and punished?

Accounts of historical crimes and trials, like the ones collected here, offer something more. They are windows on the past, revealing how our ancestors lived and the values they cherished. "Law," the eighteenth-century British jurist William Blackstone noted, "is the embodiment of the moral sentiment of the people." Crime is an offence against this moral sentiment, and a trial is staged to prove the transgression and to punish the offender. Revisiting a trial that's decades or centuries old is like prying off a lid to expose a hidden world of vice and poverty, greed and prejudice. Laws reveal how people aspired to deal with one another; crimes reveal how they really behaved, and how society controlled the worst impulses of its worst citizens. Attitudes change. The law evolves. But human nature, the past assures us, remains the same.

This collection of fifteen true tales of crime and justice has a lot to say about Nova Scotia's past. It covers more than 150 years of the province's history, from a triple-murder in 1791 at an isolated farm near Lunenburg to 1947, when Angus Walters, skipper of the racing schooner *Bluenose*, was defamed in the pages of the American magazine *Cosmopolitan*. They are drawn from communities scattered across the province, from Cape Breton Island to the renowned shipbuilding port of Lunenburg, from Amherst to the provincial capital of Halifax, from Country Harbour on the Eastern Shore to the historic town of Annapolis Royal. It's an eclectic mix of crimes and trials that caught my eye as I researched the province's legal history, yet each one has something to say about its time and place. And the themes that run through these cases – greed, vengeance, the contest between good and evil, the quest for justice – are universal.

There are stories of robbery and fraud as well as murder, along with vicious acts of piracy and two deadly disasters caused by human error. They are filled with shocking details and "the goriest of trimmings," as well as surprising twists and courtroom drama. Some of the earliest murders included here, committed long before detectives and forensic science revolutionized crime-fighting, were solved only by the discovery of seemingly trivial scraps of evidence. Since a murder conviction carried the death sentence, the defendant's life was on the line, ramping up the tension as jurors debated their verdicts. And all too often, justice was far from blind. Religious hatred, partisan rivalry, social status, poverty, ethnicity, or political corruption invaded the courtroom, threatening to upset the delicate balance between guilt and innocence.

A few of these stories have become the stuff of legend. Newspaperman Joseph Howe's 1835 libel trial, after he exposed the corrupt practices of the officials governing Halifax, is a milestone in the struggle for freedom of the press in Canada. The murders on board the ship *Saladin* before it washed up on the Nova Scotia coast in 1844 stand as one of the most atrocious acts of piracy in the Age of Sail. And James Forman may have been one of the most prolific and brazen embezzlers in history.

Most of the cases collected here, however, have been overlooked or long forgotten. The 1917 explosion that devastated Halifax is a dark chapter in the province's history, but the criminal prosecutions and hunt for scapegoats that followed are an even darker chapter in our legal history. In the 1850s Nicholas Martin was at once the most reviled and admired man in Nova Scotia; his cold-blooded killing of a judge's son sparked a debate over family honour and the legal definition of insanity. Forman's name is little-known today, but in the 1870s his greed almost destroyed one of Canada's first banks. Forgotten too is John Simon, accused on the eve of the Second World War of killing twenty-eight people by allowing his rundown hotel to become a firetrap. And Joseph Nick Thibault, the keeper of a farm used to house paupers, stood trial in 1880 for a crime so heinous that it earned the Shakespearean headline "Murder Most Foul."

Some larger-than-life characters inhabit these pages. Almost two decades after he stood trial for libel, and well into a political career that would make him premier, Joseph Howe played detective and tried to solve a homicide. A.B. MacGillivray, a wise-cracking Cape Breton judge, missed his calling as a stand-up comic. John Thompson, in one of the first cases of his illustrious career in law and politics, defended one of the men accused of murdering the captain of the ill-fated ship *Zero*. He later prosecuted Thibault for murder, served as a judge of the provincial Supreme Court, entered federal politics, and became prime minister of Canada in 1892. Brenton Halliburton, a Supreme Court judge for an astounding fifty-three years (including twenty-eight as chief justice), was on the bench when six of the cases in this collection went to trial. Underlining the intersection between law and politics in nineteenth-century Nova Scotia, Liberal politician William Young appears in several stories in a variety of roles – as defence lawyer, prosecutor, premier, and ultimately as chief justice. And Justice Benjamin Russell stood firm in the face of intense pressure – from the public, from the press, and even from his fellow judges – and refused to put innocent men behind bars in the wake of the Halifax Explosion.

An essential element of true crime, of course, is truth. My goal is to recreate the past, not to invent it. Every fact, every detail, every quotation is drawn from contemporary sources such as newspaper reports, court files, law reports, and archival records. This source material has been attributed within the text or has been cited in the Sources section.

Was justice done in all of these cases? The prosecution's evidence against many defendants seemed overwhelming, but this did not ensure they would be found guilty. For others, proof of their guilt was thin or their accusers were themselves suspects, and eager to deflect blame and escape punishment. And in many of the cases presented here, the law and the justice system were stretched to their breaking points. Under the nineteenth century's crude legal definition of insanity, was Nicholas Martin's crime an act of vengeance or the work of a madman? Did a sympathetic jury allow George Preeper, who took part in an 1850s election-day riot, to get away with murder? Was the explosion of a munitions ship in Halifax Harbour, which killed almost two thousand people, a heinous crime, as one of the city's newspapers insisted, or a tragic accident?

You be the judge.

Dean Jobb
Wolfville, Nova Scotia
May 2020

Part 1

Disorder in the Courts

Magistrate A.B. MacGillivray, Glace Bay's legendary wise-cracking judge. (Glace Bay Heritage Museum)

1

Trial by Humour

It was obvious to everyone watching the daily parade through Glace Bay police court that the eyewitness was being evasive. And that meant everyone, including the presiding magistrate. Asked repeatedly to describe an incident that left two people dead, the witness maintained he had dropped to the ground as soon as the shooting started, and saw nothing.

"I thought I was shot," he protested.

"You mean you ought to be shot," a frustrated A.B. MacGillivray snapped from the bench.

The uncomfortable witness was by no means the first person to feel the sting of MacGillivray's sharp tongue. The man who was the law in Glace Bay from the turn of the century to the Second World War – known to everyone as A.B. – produced a steady stream of one-liners at the expense of witnesses, defendants, and lawyers alike. Even now, some eighty years after his death, stories showcasing MacGillivray's caustic wit are still swapped in his native Cape Breton and beyond.

"He's a legend, the genuine article," noted Peter MacDonald, an Ontario lawyer who turned a passion for humorous courtroom stories into a literary sideline, most notably the series of Court Jesters books. "There are even children in Cape Breton who can rattle off one 'A.B.' story after another."

Like the time MacGillivray was handing down the sentence for a petty crime.

"I'm fining you $25," the magistrate began.

"Why, that's easy," the convicted man piped up. "I've got that in my arse pocket."

"... and thirty days in the county jail," MacGillivray continued, hardly missing a beat. "Have you got that in your arse pocket?"

Then there was the defence lawyer who tried MacGillivray's patience – or, more accurately, his lack of patience – with a long-winded legal argument to close out the trial of two men charged with stealing a dozen chickens. Finally, sensing that the judge might have heard enough, the lawyer stopped in mid-sentence.

"Your Honour, I hope I haven't taken up too much of your time."

"Well, I'm not going to stop you," MacGillivray replied, pulling out his pocket watch and taking a look for theatrical effect. "You can talk as long as you want. But I think you'd better know something. The longer you keep me from my dinner, the longer those tramps will roost in the county jail."

In another case, a sailor charged with drunkenness came before the Glace Bay court. The accused could speak little English and MacGillivray had a tough time extracting any useful information. Stymied, he inquired about the man's religious beliefs. Did he believe in God? The sailor indicated he didn't believe in anything.

"In that case," cracked MacGillivray, unable to resist a straight line, "I'll put you down as a Presbyterian."

* * *

The quick-witted judge who became a legend was born in the village of Grand Narrows, on the Bras d'Or Lakes, in 1858. Alexander Bernard MacGillivray was the eldest of six children whose father was a farmer and justice of the peace. By the time MacGillivray reached his teens the family had moved to Glace Bay, lured by the hope of finding jobs in the coal mines.

At age thirteen MacGillivray began working in the pits, putting in time at several collieries in the area. Then he switched to surface work, loading coal onto ships. In 1882 he married Mary Johnstone, or "Mary A.B." as she was known, to avoid confusion with the legion of other Mary MacGillivrays on the island. They raised seven children.

Along the way MacGillivray's prospects went from good to better. In 1890 he became shipping superintendent for the General Mining Company in Glace Bay. Four years later, he abandoned the coal industry for a new career. At thirty-six he was appointed magistrate for Cape Breton County. When Glace Bay was incorporated in 1901, he became the first magistrate, or lower-court judge, within the jurisdiction of the new town. He passed judgment on those charged with breaching town bylaws and minor offences such as drunkenness and shoplifting. He also presided over preliminary hearings for those facing more serious criminal charges and headed to trial in a higher court.

Legal training was not a prerequisite for the magistrate's chair in those days, and there is no evidence MacGillivray, to that point at least, had ever cracked a law book. But he looked the part of a judge. He was an imposing figure – more than six feet tall – and managed to strike a scholarly air with a carefully trimmed goatee. Vain about his appearance, he usually wore a wingtip collar and black bow tie, topping off the package with a bowler when he was not in court. But despite his formal attire, his face betrayed the jokester within. MacGillivray, his hair white with age, stares out from a surviving photograph with eyes that seem to brim with mischief.

"As he approaches the half-century mark as a magistrate," the *Cape Breton Post* observed in 1933, "A.B. still boasts the upright

A 1920s view of the coal mining town of Glace Bay, where magistrate A.B. MacGillivray held court. (Shedden Studio/Author Collection)

carriage, deep voice and cheery smile which have been lifelong characteristics."

MacGillivray held court in a small red building on Glace Bay's main street, near the railway tracks. The modest courthouse, which doubled as the judge's office, was little more than "a one-room shack," by one description. It was here that the dapper MacGillivray, the star of the show, dispensed justice and treated onlookers to his memorable punchlines.

He brought a commonsense approach to the bench, which is hardly surprising given his first-hand knowledge of hard work in the mines. "You'd find his ilk in a Lunenburg fisherman or a Halifax dockworker," recalled Leo McIntyre, a retired provincial court judge who watched MacGillivray in action in the 1930s. He had only a layman's understanding of the law, but by one account he rarely missed the mark. "In the thousands of cases which have passed through his jurisdiction," a newspaper reporter claimed near the end of MacGillivray's career, "only once has his decision been reversed by a higher court."

Absence of legal training probably explains his abiding dis-taste for lawyers. "Although he respected the lawyers who appeared before him, he was not particularly fond of them," Louis Dubinsky wrote of MacGillivray. Dubinsky, who went on to become a Nova Scotia Supreme Court judge, learned that lesson through personal experience. As a rookie lawyer, his first case was the defence of the two men charged with stealing chickens; Dubinsky was the lawyer who earned his clients a longer jail term by keeping MacGillivray from his dinner.

MacGillivray could be as crude as he was blunt. Accustomed to speaking his mind, he sometimes ruffled feathers with the earthy language he used in court. He once dismissed a lawyer's argument as "bullshit." Many of the stories that live on after him are "a little naughty," admits Peter MacDonald, who has collected numerous examples of MacGillivray's wit. "This was a man who said anything that popped into his head." MacGillivray was fluent in the Gaelic of his ancestors, prompting one wag to suggest the magistrate was able to speak three languages: "The English language on the bench, Gaelic when with his Scottish friends, and bad language when he's riled."

But MacGillivray, warts and all, is best remembered for his mastery of a fourth language – humour. It's difficult to establish if all the A.B. stories are true, and one suspects several are embellished or were attributed to him over the years as his reputation grew. Many A.B. stories, Dubinsky claimed, were "figments of the teller's imagination."

He swore, however, that one classic line did come from Mac-Gillivray's lips. A man charged with possession of stolen goods, the story goes, appeared for trial without a lawyer – certainly no handicap in MacGillivray's court. After the prosecution rested its case, the defendant was adamant that he had not realized the items in question were stolen. MacGillivray asked the man if he had anything to say to sum up his case. With that, the accused jumped to his feet and shouted: "As God is my judge, I am not guilty."

MacGillivray must have flashed his mischievous grin as he delivered a punchline and verdict rolled into one.

"He's not. I am. And you are."

* * *

Leo McIntyre, an unabashed MacGillivray fan, lamented that characters such as A.B. are few and far between today. Then again, it can be argued that judicial office should be the preserve of those with legal training and a sense of fairness and public service, not stand-up comics. MacGillivray's antics did little to enhance the image of the province's lowest court. A Nova Scotia politician who was a younger contemporary of MacGillivray, Gordon Rompkey, once remarked that the greatest accomplishment of too many magistrates was the production of "tales" that were "good for a laugh."

Wisecracks notwithstanding, there were those who felt some proceedings in the magistrate's court were no laughing matter. Besides lacking legal training, magistrates were allowed, even expected, to supplement their income through court costs levied on top of the fines they imposed. And that created the appearance, if not the reality, that defendants were being convicted not on the weight of the evidence, but to line a magistrate's pockets.

As early as 1916, an opposition politician rose in the provincial legislature and charged that "four-fifths of the practising magistrates in Cape Breton were crooked and dishonest." The proof, he charged, was the fact that few had filed the required reports with the government disclosing fines and penalties imposed in their courts. *The Halifax Herald*, a newspaper bitterly opposed to the Liberal party then in power, used the outburst to condemn the situation in Cape Breton's magistrates' courts as "nothing short of a public scandal." Names were never put to the allegation, but it's likely MacGillivray, a Liberal appointee, was lumped in with the tainted majority.

The government ignored the allegations as grandstanding, and nothing was done. By the early 1930s Justice W.L. Hall, a Supreme Court judge and a former provincial attorney general, was attacking the fee-collection system as "absolutely vicious." He called for the firing of all sitting magistrates and their replacement with lawyers paid only a salary.

The provincial government was finally prodded into action in 1938. A new act created the post of "police magistrate," responsible for adjudicating cases previously in the magistrates' domain. The new court officers were forbidden from taking fees, and legal training was finally recognized as an asset; they were required to have practised law in Nova Scotia for at least three years. Legal scholars hailed the long-overdue changes as "the greatest advance in the administration of law in Nova Scotia" in more than fifty years.

MacGillivray, now nearly an octogenarian, and other holdovers from the earlier era were allowed to serve out their time. Three years later, and forty-seven years after taking his place on the bench, MacGillivray retired in 1941. He died of a stroke two years later at eighty-four. A sense of humour will never be a barrier to judicial office, but it's unlikely MacGillivray's legacy of courtroom one-liners will ever be rivalled.

2

"An Unshackled Press"

The incendiary letter published in *The Novascotian* that New Year's Day accused Halifax's most powerful public officials of corruption. Signed with the pseudonym "The People," it alleged that each year £1,000 was being looted from "the poor and distressed" and "pocketed by men whose services the country might well spare" – namely the dozen magistrates responsible for governing the city. These officials, the letter alleged, had been fleecing the public "by one stratagem or other" for the previous three decades, a haul of roughly £30,000. It was an astronomical sum in 1835.

The magistrates, furious at being exposed in the press, urged Nova Scotia's attorney general to launch a libel prosecution. The target of their wrath was *The Novascotian*'s upstart, thirty-year-old proprietor, Joseph Howe. He hadn't written the letter – it had been submitted by one of his friends, George Thompson – but this made no difference. As the newspaper's editor, Howe was responsible for its contents. He was charged with criminal libel, accused of "wickedly, maliciously and seditiously desiring and intending to stir up and excite discontent among His Majesty's subjects." If convicted, he faced a heavy fine or a lengthy prison term.

Within weeks, Howe stood before a jury and single-handedly mounted a counterattack. His trial stands as a landmark in Nova Scotia history. No guided tour of Province House, the legislature building in Halifax, is complete without a stop at the ornate library, the scene of this courtroom showdown, where a bronze plaque marks the event. Overnight, the trial made Howe a political force to be reckoned with, signalling the beginning of a political career that would thrust him into the forefront of the battle for responsible government and, later, the fight against Canada's formation in 1867. The trial also marked the end of the line for the corrupt magistrates whose misdeeds he had laid bare.

Later generations would come to regard Howe's trial as a watershed, establishing the principle of freedom of the press in Canada. But the case did not rewrite the draconian laws governing how nineteenth-century journalists did their jobs. Howe's real legacy was showing that one person, armed with a belief in the truth and convinced of the rightness of his cause, could do battle with the powers that be – and triumph.

* * *

In the 1830s, local government in Nova Scotia was in the hands of magistrates appointed by the colonial administration. In Halifax, the colonial capital and largest city, magistrates (this was before lower-court judges assumed the title) supervised the operation of the police department, poor asylum, and other public institutions. Below the magistrates in the evolving bureaucracy were grand jurors – middle-class property owners chosen by lot to keep tabs on the magistrates. By the time Howe became a member of the grand jury in 1832, that body was beginning to take the magistrates to task for the sorry state of many government services.

Howe outlined some of the abuses in the course of his trial. The magistrate in charge of the city prison had turned the institution into his private preserve; he stored vegetables in the cells, stabled his horse in the woodshed, and forced inmates to make shoes for his family. The poor asylum – the last refuge for those down on their luck – received inferior, overpriced supplies under the management of its director, another magistrate. By the latter part of 1834, *The Novascotian* had begun a print campaign against the corrupt practices of the magistrates. The war of words culminated in the no-holds-barred letter of January 1, 1835.

After the libel charge was laid, Howe consulted several lawyers. They were unanimously of the opinion that he had no defence. The law of the time was clear: publication of anything that was intended to disturb the public peace or injure the reputations of individuals was libellous and a crime. What if the allegations were true? In the eyes of the law, this meant nothing. The sole issue for the jury to decide was whether the libel amounted to a breach of the peace.

Here lay Howe's only hope. If he could prove his allegations, then it followed that he had not published the offending letter with the intention of breaching the peace. Technically speaking, this was still libel, but it was the kind of argument that might sway a jury. Gathering evidence to support the charges against the magistrates turned out to be easy. An appeal for help published in another newspaper, the *Acadian Recorder*, did the trick. The next day, Howe recalled, throngs of people crammed his office, "every one of whom had suffered some exaction, had some complaint to expose, or had had justice denied or delayed."

There's an old saying that anyone who represents themselves in court has a fool for a client. But since the law was not on his side, Howe decided he'd rather be foolish than give up. If he had "the nerve and power to put the whole case before a jury," he reasoned, "and they were fair and reasonable men, they must acquit."

* * *

Newspaperman Joseph Howe stood trial on a charge of criminal libel in 1835 in the Supreme Court chamber of Province House in Halifax. (Author photograph)

The trial opened on March 2, 1835, in the Supreme Court chamber in Province House – a small room that seems larger thanks to a high ceiling. Balconies lined three of the four walls to accommodate spectators and the judges' bench squatted in front of high windows that overlooked Halifax's bustling Hollis Street. The room was "crammed to overflowing" with onlookers, Howe noted, and "hot as a furnace." A number of judges joined the presiding jurist, Chief Justice Brenton Halliburton, on the bench as advisors and observers. From them, Howe expected little. His best hope rested with the jurors, and as luck would have it, five of the twelve had served with Howe on the grand jury. They knew, as he knew, how the magistrates were abusing their positions.

James F. Gray, a senior Halifax lawyer, acted for the Crown and delivered the prosecution's opening address. "It is impossible for the jury to say there is not sufficient defamatory, malicious matter in this letter to constitute libel," he said. In other words, their only option was to convict Howe as charged. Another newspaperman was called as a witness to confirm that the letter had been published, but this became a formality when Howe acknowledged he had printed it. The letter from "The People" was then read into the court record, and the prosecutor closed his case. He had only to prove that the alleged libel had been published, and that the words amounted to libel.

Now it was Howe's turn. He had pored over books on libel law for a week to try to hammer out a defence, and had spent another week preparing a speech to the jury. One observer has suggested he benefited from the lack of professional legal help. Judges have traditionally bent over backwards to appear fair to anyone unable – or unwilling, in Howe's case – to retain a lawyer. Howe's biographer, the Dalhousie University political scientist J. Murray Beck, pointed out that a lawyer would have been limited to arguing the law, which was definitely not on the side of this accused. Howe could "come up with an unorthodox defence and, as a layman, be given wide leeway to use it."

He did. For more than six hours Howe marshalled his case, turning the courtroom into a forum to expose fresh examples of abuse among the high and mighty. He cited case after case of corrupt practices by the magistrates, singling out some of the worst offenders by name. Those with ringside seats to the trial made no secret of whose side they were on – Chief Justice Halliburton was forced to ask spectators to keep their applause to a minimum. Then Howe took his arguments to a higher plane. He pleaded that Nova Scotia's newspapers should receive "the same rational protection" being afforded the press in Britain, where juries were less likely to hand down libel convictions when official corruption was exposed.

"Your verdict will be the most important in its consequences ever delivered before this tribunal," he predicted, challenging the jurors "to leave an unshackled press as a legacy to your children." It was a masterful performance, all the more remarkable because Howe, to that point, had rarely spoken in public. One juryman was reportedly moved to tears.

A plaque at the foot of Howe's statue outside Province House portrays his rousing speech to the jury. (Author photograph)

Howe's long speech made it impossible to finish the trial that day. Next morning, Attorney General Samuel Archibald summed up the Crown's case. If ever there was a tough act to follow, this was it, and Archibald made no attempt to match Howe's oratory. He warned the jury that much of what they had heard the previous day was hearsay – second-hand evidence – and no lawyer would have been allowed to go to such lengths.

Chief Justice Halliburton, the target of some of Howe's journalistic barbs in the past, left no doubt where he stood as he closed the case. "In my opinion the paper charged is a libel, and your duty is to state by your verdict that it is libelous," he bluntly told the jurors. But, he added half-heartedly, "you are not bound by my opinion. You are not to be influenced by my feelings, but to pronounce upon the case before you according to the sober convictions of your own minds."

It took the jurors just ten minutes to apply their "sober convictions" and return a verdict of not guilty. Cheers echoed through the Supreme Court chamber and the celebration spilled onto the snow-covered streets of Halifax. Supporters formed their sleighs into a victory parade. But there was little joy among the city's scandal-tainted magistrates; within days of the verdict, six resigned. The post was so thoroughly discredited that the government had a tough time finding anyone willing to take their place. Howe had solidified his reputation as champion of the common man. His gutsy performance in the courtroom was the springboard for a political career that would one day lead him to the premier's office.

* * *

"It is often stated that Howe established the freedom of the press through his acquittal," Beck wrote of the trial. "This is a myth that has little basis in fact." Howe did nothing to discourage the myth-making – in the first edition of *The Novascotian* published in the wake of the trial, he boldly declared that "the press of Nova Scotia is free."

Some historians jumped on the bandwagon and gave credence to Howe's inflated view of the trial. Wilfred Kesterton, in his history of Canadian journalism, described Howe's trial as "the most momentous freedom-of-the-press precedent" of the early nineteenth century. But the case of The King versus Howe did nothing to ease the strict laws that governed what newspaper editors could publish without risking a criminal prosecution. A 1980s report of the Law Reform Commission of Canada, which called for the abolition of the outdated offence of criminal libel, traced the development of Canadian libel law without even mentioning Howe's finest hour.

"The law is not changed by the verdicts of juries," explained Joseph Chisholm, a Nova Scotia chief justice who was among Howe's greatest admirers. But, he acknowledged, "it is sometimes disregarded by juries in their verdicts."

An accommodating jury rescued Howe, but his brilliant defence left a legacy even though the verdict did not rewrite the law. The trial showed the folly of using the criminal courts to stifle dissent in the press. By prosecuting Howe, the government unwittingly gave him a public platform to hammer away at the corrupt practices of the magistrates. And the jury's acquittal served notice that the public would not tolerate such abuses.

Howe's prosecution was not the last for criminal libel in Canada, but it undoubtedly helped speed up the trend toward settling libel claims through the civil courts, punishing libellous press reports with awards of monetary damages rather than the spectre of prison. A lawsuit was still an effective check on the printing of unfounded allegations, though. Howe's successor at the helm of *The Novascotian*, Richard Nugent, was bankrupted by damages awarded in a series of libel suits in the early 1840s.

While Howe did not change the libel law, the law was changing. In 1843 the British Parliament passed an amendment allowing newspaper publishers to claim the truth of a statement as a defence to libel, providing they could show the statement was published for the public good. It would be another three decades before Canadian lawmakers followed suit and enacted similar provisions. Libel is still on the books as a crime in Canada, despite the Law Reform Commission's recommendation that it be abolished. But thanks to Howe's bravery, it has been decades since the criminal law was used to try to silence a journalist.

3

Death at the Waterloo Tavern

The noisy taverns and brothels of Halifax's notorious Barrack Street area were closing down as city watchmen John Shehan and Maurice Power made their rounds. It was a few minutes past midnight on a damp, overcast September night in 1853. Suddenly, Thomas Murphy ran up to the officers.

"Come quickly," he shouted. "A man has jumped out of a window of my house."

With the watchmen at his heels, Murphy ran back to the Waterloo, the tavern he operated in the shadow of the Citadel, Halifax's star-shaped, hilltop fortress. A sailor, a crewman from a British warship anchored in the harbour, was sprawled at the foot of the staircase leading into the tavern; his head, bloody from cuts above each eye, rested on the bottom step. Broken glass and a hat, handkerchief, and a pair of shoes littered the sidewalk. There were no signs of life.

Shehan was told the man had jumped or fallen from one of the tavern's upper windows, but the watchman was unconvinced. "It appeared to me that if he had jumped … he would not be lying in the position he was," Shehan explained. Besides, the window was not directly above where the body had come to rest; it was at least nine feet to one side.

Shehan hoisted the body onto his back and carried it down George Street to the police station on the waterfront. There, Dr. James Allan made a quick examination and declared the sailor dead. The sketchy facts Shehan had gathered at the scene were not adding up. Murphy had told him that John Gordon, a carpenter rooming at the tavern, had been upstairs in bed when the sailor fell to his death. But Gordon, when questioned separately by Shehan's partner, Power, claimed he had been downstairs, in Murphy's room, when the sailor died. Why was one of them lying?

There was one way to get to the bottom of things. Murphy, who had accompanied Shehan to the police station, was placed under arrest. The watchmen returned to the Waterloo and rounded up the remaining occupants until a coroner's inquest could determine whether the death was an accident, a suicide, or a crime.

It was the start of a murder case that would expose the seamy underside of Nova Scotia's capital city – and cause a courtroom uproar like few others in the province's history.

* * *

Alexander Allan and several other crewmen of HMS *Cumberland* had rowed ashore about suppertime on September 7 for a night on the town. Allan was about twenty-five and described as powerful and muscular, with a head of thick, curly black hair. "He was a very sober, industrious, steady young man" in the estimation of one of his shipmates. He had served on *Cumberland* for about three years and sworn off liquor as he neared the end of his tour of duty. Another crewman recollected that he had only seen Allan drunk once in the previous six months. But Allan had a reputation as a scrapper and, drunk or sober, he was usually up for a fight.

The sailors headed straight for "The Hill" – the name given the bars and houses of ill-repute that served the army barracks surrounding the Citadel. "Here gathered an evil slum of grog sellers, pimps, and prostitutes," Nova Scotia author Thomas Raddall wrote in his history of Halifax, *Warden of the North*. There was no shortage of similar establishments on the waterfront that catered to the Royal Navy, but Raddall noted that sailors sometimes ventured the half-dozen blocks inland to Barrack Street, where encounters with soldiers often ended in fights. "They never can agree," one seafarer said of army and navy men.

All this drinking, carousing, and fighting did not sit well with Halifax's upper classes. Argyle Street, midway up Citadel Hill and sandwiched between the waterfront and Barrack Street, boasted the fine homes of some of the city's wealthiest citizens. And the blight was spreading. In an October 1853 letter to *The Novascotian* newspaper, a writer complained that Grafton Street, just a block above Argyle, "has become an abominable den of prostitutes ... and a nuisance and annoyance to the respectable Citizens residing in that neighbourhood."

The first stop for Allan and company was the Waterloo. Murphy had been in business for six years and kept out of trouble with the law by closing on time and barring youths from the premises. He claimed he sold "nothing but liquor," and officials turned a blind eye to Murphy's profitable sideline: four prostitutes occupied the upstairs rooms.

Allan was at the Waterloo between six and seven o'clock and apparently drank only ginger beer. About eight, he met up with another *Cumberland* crewman, Anthony Bainbridge, at another tavern, but cleared out after a scuffle with a group of soldiers wielding sticks. Allan then went looking for his former girlfriend, Margaret Murphy.

Described by one tavernkeeper as a "common prostitute" and "a woman addicted to drinking," she was the estranged wife of the owner of the Waterloo. Margaret and Thomas Murphy had been separated for about five years, and during the summer of 1852 she and Allan had lived together. The liaison had caused bitterness between the two men. "Murphy seemed to have a spite against him," noted one sailor – and a possible motive for murder. Murphy had once thrown Allan out of the Waterloo, uttering a vague threat to "give him what he had promised him a long time ago."

Allan was no longer living with Margaret Murphy by the summer of 1853, but he was outraged to find her at Young's Tavern in the company of one of his shipmates, Peter Lawrie. Allan called Lawrie into the street but got the worst of the fight and ended up lying in a gutter, bleeding from a small cut above one eye. After passersby helped him to his feet, Allan shook hands with Lawrie, who insisted they "parted friends." Margaret Murphy stayed with Lawrie, and Allan, who seemed to have a nose for trouble, headed back to the Waterloo.

He arrived shortly after eleven. There were two versions of what happened next, one told by a sailor and the other by Thomas Murphy and his compatriots. William Giles of the *Cumberland* later testified that a fiddler was playing and he and Allan danced with two of the women, then treated them to a drink at the bar. Allan's generosity seems to have enraged Murphy, who "told him to clear out, or by God he would give him what he had promised him that six weeks past." But Giles's story did not stack up in one respect – he insisted there was no blood on Allan's face. Other witnesses said blood could be seen coming from the wound Allan suffered earlier in the street fight.

Murphy's account was more suspicious. He denied even knowing Allan's name prior to the sailor's arrival at the Waterloo on September 7. Murphy said he was just about to close for the night when Allan entered and had a drink at the bar. His face was bleeding badly and he seemed "confused in his mind." Murphy suggested he go upstairs and have one of the women wash off the blood. "The last words he spoke to me were, 'Tom, I am sorry to have been used this way by my shipmates.'" Murphy swore he was writing in his room about thirty minutes later when he heard glass break and found Allan's body on the stairs.

The other occupants of the tavern – Mary Ann Cole, Matilda Ballard, Sarah Myers, who were prostitutes; a servant, David Parsons; and the boarder, John Gordon – told similar stories at the coroner's inquest convened the day after the death. But a doctor who examined the body testified there was "no doubt" Allan's death "was caused by violence" and not a fall. The coroner's jury, composed of six sailors and six civilians in the interest of fairness, seemed convinced that everyone was lying to protect themselves and the killer or killers. Despite the lack of any evidence implicating anyone, the jury's verdict accused Murphy, Gordon, Cole, Parsons, Ballard, and Myers of murder. The six were jailed pending trial.

* * *

Allan's death strained the already tense relations between the military men stationed in Halifax and their civilian hosts. City officials, fearing his shipmates would seek revenge and trash the Waterloo, swore in about seventy special constables on September 8, the day after Allan was killed. The local military commander agreed to cancel shore leave to help to defuse the situation.

The incident also brought calls for a crackdown on vice. "Why are these fearful dens of iniquity suffered to exist?" fumed *The British Colonist*. "It is believed that many a murder is committed in them. Occasionally on the clearing out of a well, or after a fire, a body has been found. Why do not the Aldermen make a clean sweep, and clear out the wretches who turn our city into a Gomorrah? ... If the house of Murphy is allowed again to be tenanted by a brothel keeper," the newspaper warned, "it will be a vile disgrace."

Meanwhile, the united front erected by the six suspects began to crumble. James Wilson, the city jailer, knew Cole and spoke to her briefly before she was locked up. "Mary, has it come to this?" he asked. "I had nothing to do with it," she replied, bursting into tears. "I was in Tom's room when they were upstairs killing the man." Cole would say no more and later denied making the statement.

Form of appointment of Special Constables under Act, 1853.

CITY OF HALIFAX, S.S.

Be it remembered that on this Eighth day of September, in the year of our Lord One Thousand Eight Hundred and Fifty Three, We, William George Anderson, Alderman of the City of Halifax, and acting as Mayor of said City, in the absence of the Mayor, under resolution of the City Council, Benjamin William Salter, Bernard O'Neill and Richard Nugent, three of the Aldermen of said City—entertaining just apprehension of riot and disturbance in said City, in consequence of the death of a Seaman of the Royal Navy, recently found dead at or near the Waterloo Tavern, in Barrack Street, in said City, kept by one Thomas Murphy, said Seaman being suspected to have been unlaw- fully slain, Do hereby appoint the several persons, whose names are contained in the annexed list, to act as Special Constables within said City, for the space of fourteen days from this date, unless their appoint- ment be sooner revoked, to assist in preserving peace and order within said City ;—under, and by virtue of, an Act of this Province of Nova Scotia, passed in the present year, entitled " an Act respecting Special Constables."

Given under our hands, at Halifax aforesaid, the day and year first before written

W. G. ANDERSON, Acting Mayor.
B. W. SALTER,   Alderman.
BERNARD O'NEILL,   "
RICHARD NUGENT,   "

We approve of the above.
ARCH. SCOTT,
ROB. NOBLE,
A. PRIMROSE.

N. B. About 70 citizens were sworn and acted under this.

Seventy special constables were sworn in to keep the peace after a Royal Navy sailor was found dead outside Halifax's Waterloo Tavern in 1853. (Beamish Murdoch, *Supplement to the Charter and Ordinances of the City of Halifax*, 1854)

During the fall of 1853 Joseph Howe, the provincial secretary, visited the jail. It was an official visit, prompted by complaints that the facility was not secure. Howe, a champion of press freedom and democratic reform, proved to be adept at cracking a murder case. The jailer introduced Howe to Myers and Ballard during the tour. Weeks later, they asked to see the famous politician. Myers thought he was "the fittest man" to hear what she and Ballard had to say. Howe maintained he "said nothing to induce the confession made by the girls; I made them no promise." But, he assured them, "in the event of their telling all they knew they would be protected by the government from injury."

Myers, twenty-three, and Ballard, nineteen, told a similar story. Myers had taken Allan upstairs to her room to wash his face at a basin, then returned to the bar, where she was chatting with Ballard and Parsons when they heard a noise upstairs. Ballard said it sounded like "shuffling feet." Then Myers described a cry "as if a man was struck over the head by someone."

The women and Parsons went to the door leading to the street and saw Murphy and Gordon dragging Allan down the stairs. Gordon had him by the waist, Murphy held him by the throat. Allan "was not struggling – he seemed to be pretty well gone," said Myers. Ballard, however, swore that the sailor continued to screech as he was carried outside. Then Gordon struck Allan on the head with something – neither woman could tell what it was – and returned inside.

When Murphy entered, his hands were covered with blood. He ordered the women to their rooms. "If you say a word about this," he warned, "I will take your life as I did that of the sailor." Fearful that Murphy would make good on his threat, Ballard and Myers admitted they had lied at the coroner's inquest.

The prosecution dropped charges against the women in return for their testimony at the upcoming trial. They remained behind bars but their treatment improved, and Myers was even paid ten shillings a month to work in the jailer's kitchen. At trial, defence lawyers would hint that such treatment was a strong motive to lie about how Allan had died.

Joseph Howe, Nova Scotia's provincial secretary, was touring the Halifax jail when a chance encounter made him a key witness in a murder trial. (William Notman/McCord Museum I-16720.1)

Four people were still accused of killing Allan. A grand jury reviewed the evidence, including the women's statements, later that fall and ordered Murphy and Gordon to stand trial for murder. The charge against Parsons and Cole was reduced to being an accessory after the fact to murder, for harbouring the other two after the crime was committed.

* * *

The trial opened before the Supreme Court on April 21, 1854. The presiding judge was Thomas Chandler Haliburton, whose literary creation, the fast-talking Yankee pedlar Sam Slick, had already made him an internationally known satirist. "As a judge, Haliburton was conscientious, upright, intelligent, adhering to the spirit rather than to the letter of the law," wrote one biographer. "He was, however, in no sense a great judge, and his propensity for punning and his strong sense of the ludicrous, although often enlivening an otherwise dull courtroom session, did not add to his reputation."

The circumstances of Allan's death ensured this trial would be anything but dull. In his opening address to the jury, William Young, a diminutive Scottish-born politician who had assumed the posts of premier and attorney general earlier in the month, cautioned that the trial would reveal "a scene from which, it is true, few communities like this are exempt – but which, when brought distinctly and vividly before us, pain and shock the moral sense of every right-thinking man." Young also candidly admitted that his case rested on the word of two women whose character "may not be all we could wish."

The trial lasted three days. Dr. Allan, who first examined the body (and was not related to the victim), attributed the death to a massive fracture extending from the top of the head to the base of the skull. "It must have been caused by some heavy and tremendous blow," he testified, probably inflicted with a flat instrument.

The defence, led by future premier James W. Johnston, suggested the sailor could have received the injury in a fall. "A man jumping out of the window in question," the doctor insisted, "could not have sustained those injuries." Even Haliburton seemed to doubt Dr. Allan's testimony. Could a man receive such an injury in a fall, the judge asked, and still move nine feet – the distance Allan was lying to one side of the window – before dying? "It was possible," the doctor replied, "but not at all probable."

Then the prosecution produced an eyewitness – Richard Powell, a Hants County farmer who had been in Halifax on September 7 to sell produce. As he walked along Barrack Street about midnight, he testified, two men emerged from the door of the Waterloo Tavern and threw another man down the stairs. Then he claimed he heard someone cry, "Murder." Powell said he did not come forward at the coroner's inquest because "I wanted to keep out of trouble." He admitted the government had paid him a small sum to cover his travel expenses to appear at the trial.

Johnston, regarded as one of the best public speakers of his time, made short work of Powell on cross-examination. After establishing that Powell was a habitual drinker ("I take a horn of grog whenever I can catch it," he confessed), Johnston deftly poked holes in his testimony. Powell responded by being evasive and making jokes, twice drawing rebukes from the bench. By the time the defence lawyer was finished, Powell's evidence appeared useless.

Myers and Ballard appeared before the jury and repeated their statements implicating Murphy and Gordon. Myers stood up well under defence questioning, but one newspaper reporter noted that Ballard seemed confused during Johnston's lengthy and detailed cross-examination. After calling Joseph Howe to outline the circumstances of the confessions, Young rested the prosecution's case.

The defence opened by seeking a verdict of not guilty for Cole and Parsons, since there was no evidence they acted as accessories. Haliburton granted the request, and the two were released.

In those days persons accused of crimes could not testify; Cole and Parsons could now take the witness stand for the remaining defendants, Murphy and Gordon.

The evidence of John Patterson, the first defence witness, created a sensation in the courtroom. After a day of fishing on a nearby inlet called the Northwest Arm, he returned to the city about midnight on September 7 and saw a man hanging by his hands from a window ledge of the Waterloo. The man fell onto the stairs below, and someone came out the front door, said, "Good God, I believe the man is dead," and ran off after a watchman. Patterson, who lived in the small Halifax County community of Terence Bay, said he had never been inside the tavern and did not know either Murphy or Gordon.

The prosecutor questioned why Patterson had not come forward earlier. "I did not tell at the outset because the girls first told the right story, that the man had fallen from the window," Patterson replied, standing his ground. "I only came forward when I heard they had contradicted their own testimony and sworn that Gordon and Murphy murdered the man ... Any one who swears that this was the case lies."

Parsons was next. He denied that he, Myers, and Ballard had seen Murphy and Gordon carry Allan down the stairs. "The whole story of Ballard and Myers is a lie from beginning to end," he claimed. Parsons, Gordon, and Murphy found Allan's body lying on the stairs, he testified, and Murphy ran for the watchmen.

Haliburton had heard enough. He took the unusual step of interrupting the trial and went into a huddle at the front of the courtroom with the attorney general and Chief Justice Brenton Halliburton and Justice William Blowers Bliss, two other judges who were on the bench as observers. Young returned to his place and the trial judge, Haliburton, repeated their discussions for the record. In light of the "very contradictory testimony," he said, "I am sure no jury would feel themselves justified in convicting the prisoners." Young agreed that the prosecution's case, already "clouded with suspicion" in his opinion because two of his chief witnesses were prostitutes, had been crippled by the contradictory stories told by Patterson and Parsons. "I think the case should here conclude," he said.

Chief Justice Halliburton – who was no relation to the trial judge, despite their similar surnames – broke in. "In a capital case, where the lives of the parties arraigned are at stake upon testimony so contradictory and conflicting, no jury could feel themselves at liberty, and no Judge would be authorized under such circumstances in instructing them to convict." Having judges sitting in on trials, a common practice at the time, had its advantages; Bliss agreed, in effect giving an appeal court's stamp of approval on the spot.

Justice Haliburton asked the jurors to stand. "Whether the unfortunate man Allan met his death by some act of folly or madness of his own or whether his life was taken by the prisoners at the bar or by any other persons is enveloped in mystery – so entire and so complete that human judgement is baffled," he explained. "I have therefore to recommend gentlemen that you return a verdict of not guilty." The jurors held a brief discussion without leaving the room and acquitted Murphy and Gordon.

The judge, however, refused to let the men completely off the hook. Their escape was "a fortunate one," Justice Haliburton reminded the pair, based on "the Providential production of certain counter-testimony." Then he launched into a lecture. Gordon, a man able to support himself with a trade, had chosen to live in a brothel "as a bully or a partner." Murphy had degraded himself "below the dignity of manhood to engage in the occupation almost of a beast." He admonished both men to seek an honest calling and chided Halifax authorities for granting licences for the sale of liquor in brothels such as the Waterloo.

* * *

How Alexander Allan met his death would remain shrouded in a web of lies and accusations. The evils of Barrack Street, thrown into stark relief by the trial, persisted for at least another decade. In 1870, *The Morning Chronicle* reported, the area still featured "scenes of drunkenness and riot requiring the largest part of the policeman's time." But the military issued an order in May of that year banning sailors and soldiers from the Barrack Street area. Taverns and brothels, robbed of their clientele, closed or moved to other parts of the city.

As for the Waterloo Tavern, it was eventually torn down and replaced with a brick building devoted to more exalted pursuits as the site of the Salvation Army Citadel. And the street itself was given a new name – Brunswick Street – to help erase the stigma of its sordid past.

Part 2

Breaking the Bank

4

Cooking the Books

It could have been called the Bank of Forman. James Forman had been running the Bank of Nova Scotia for close to four decades – since the institution was founded in 1832, to be precise. As cashier, he was in charge of operations at the bank's main office, only a stone's throw away from the bustling wharves that were the lifeblood of Halifax's economy. Forman did the bookkeeping, using a quill pen and leather-bound ledgers to keep track of money held on deposit, loaned to local businessmen, or tied up in the gold and silver reserves that backed the bank's paper money. The bank was one of the largest financial institutions in the Maritime Provinces; by 1870 slightly more than $2.1 million in assets – a staggering amount at the time – was under Forman's direct control.

Forman, who turned seventy-five that year, could have inspired the term "hands-on manager." Stooped with age, with a salt-and-pepper beard, baggy eyes, and his remaining hair combed only by the wind, Forman could have been mistaken for an elderly customer who had wandered behind the wickets. But his face bore an expression as mean as a bulldog's, and few questioned his orders. And he was not just another employee. While he was only

James Forman early in his banking career. He had been the Bank of Nova Scotia's head cashier of the for almost forty years by 1870, when an audit exposed his massive fraud. (McCord Museum I-9720.0.1)

a notch above the lowly clerks in the bank's hierarchy, he vastly outstripped them in social standing. Like the merchants and lawyers who served on the bank's board of directors, he lived in a posh estate amidst the quiet, tree-lined streets of the city's South End.

Besides being the bank's most powerful and longest-serving employee, Forman was its most trusted. He had his own set of keys to the vault, a privilege enjoyed by only one other official, the president. And rather than being saddled with the mundane task of tabulating figures at the office, Forman was free to pack up the bank's books and work on them at home in the evenings. No one dared question such unusual practices, not even the directors who took turns working weekly stints at the bank.

Forman had the complete confidence of the man at the bank's helm, his close friend Mather Byles Almon. President since 1837, Almon was a wealthy Halifax merchant and one of the bank's founders. He was also agent for the General Mining Association, which had exclusive rights to mine Nova Scotia coal – a lucrative account that Almon had brought into the bank's fold. Over the years he had come to rely heavily on Forman, who was two years his senior and had been with the bank as long as anyone could remember. By 1870, with Almon's health failing and his eyesight nearly gone, the reliance upon Forman's judgment and integrity was complete.

So it was an act of immense bravery when a junior clerk by the name of Johns approached the bank's accountant, James Mackintosh, one day in the spring of 1870 to point out something in the books that just didn't add up. By his reckoning, a large sum – about $30,000 – was unaccounted for. Johns had "looked upon it as an error for over a month," and said nothing. But after repeated attempts to reconcile the figures, the clerk later noted, "there was enough to satisfy me there was a false entry."

The revelation confirmed suspicions Mackintosh had been harbouring about his boss. He knew Forman's personal account at the bank had been overdrawn for some time. For the past couple of years, he had been carrying out a clandestine audit of the figures Forman had recorded at the end of each banking day. But since

Forman alone made the entries, Mackintosh had little luck determining if they matched the money flowing through the bank's coffers.

Now, it appeared, Forman had become sloppy. After taking a couple of months to recheck his math and summon his own courage, Mackintosh went to Almon in July 1870 to report serious discrepancies in the books. But $30,000 was only the tip of the iceberg – Forman had been systematically looting the Bank of Nova Scotia's vault for at least twenty-five years, helping himself to more than ten times that amount. A junior clerk's sharp eye proved to be the beginning of the end for one of the most prolific embezzlers of all time.

* * *

The Bank of Nova Scotia was a pillar of the province's financial community – the institution where successful businessmen like shipping magnate Samuel Cunard kept their accounts. But when it had come into being a generation earlier, in the 1830s, it had been an upstart, the nemesis of Halifax's business and political elite. In fact, it was created for the sole purpose of challenging that clique's stranglehold on local commerce.

By the early 1800s, Nova Scotia's economy – based on farming, fishing, shipbuilding, and overseas trade – was mature enough to support a bank. Merchants required a source of credit, and there was a desperate need for some form of currency that was acceptable to all. Gold and silver coins, be they Spanish doubloons or British sovereigns, were considered the best form of legal tender, but few merchants wanted to cart around tubs of coins as they went about their business.

The solution was a bank that could loan money and put its own notes in circulation, backed by gold and silver held in its vaults. Four times, between 1801 and 1825, Nova Scotia lawmakers were asked to incorporate a bank; each proposal was defeated due to a clause making the proposed bank a monopoly. Politicians in rural areas of the province balked at putting all this commercial power in the hands of a single institution based in Halifax.

What the city's business leaders were denied by legislation, however, they managed to create by agreement. In 1825, shortly after the final incorporation attempt failed, eight wealthy Haligonians banded together to form the Halifax Banking Company. The leading lights included Enos Collins, a merchant and shipper reputed to be the richest man in British North America. The new bank set up shop in a corner of a Collins-owned stone warehouse on the waterfront, and became known as Collins' Bank. (The word BANK can still be seen inscribed above the doorway of its former premises, now part of the Historic Properties heritage district). The only difference between the private bank and the institutions proposed earlier was the lack of a public charter. The monopoly over banking, so long thwarted by suspicious politicians, was now a fact.

Resentment over the Halifax Banking Company's power soon renewed calls for the creation of a public bank. Many merchants and businessmen were incensed with the bank's policies, which included redeeming the bulk of its notes in government-issued paper money instead of prized gold and silver. Reform-minded politicians such as James Boyle Uniacke led the campaign for a competing bank while Joseph Howe cheered their efforts in the pages of his feisty newspaper, *The Novascotian*.

After scores of potential investors signed on, a bill to incorporate the Bank of Nova Scotia went before the provincial legislature in 1832. After a stormy debate, the bill cleared the House of Assembly by a healthy margin and was forwarded to the Legislative Council – the appointed upper house of the legislature – for approval. The chances of winning the council's endorsement seemed bleak: five of its twelve members were partners in the Halifax Banking Company. One backer of the new bank believed the Man in the Moon was more likely than the council to approve the bill.

To no one's surprise, the bill came back amended to death. Onerous restrictions tacked on by the council threatened to stop the Bank of Nova Scotia in its tracks. But the howls of outrage in the assembly and the Halifax press eventually convinced the council to temper the worst of its amendments. The bank, saddled with only a handful of new rules governing capital reserves and increasing the liability of its directors, was incorporated on March 30, 1832.

The first board of directors went about starting a bank from scratch with a serious handicap – no one involved had hands-on banking experience. Banknotes were ordered from American printers and a newspaper advertisement was placed seeking a suitable building in the centre of town. But the most important step was hiring the key employee, the cashier.

A committee of directors chose Forman, a thirty-seven-year-old businessman whose credentials were backed by his family's good standing in Halifax society. Forman's father, James, had been a partner in a profitable Halifax wholesaling house that specialized in wine, and was among the backers of the first failed attempt to establish a bank three decades earlier. He had joined the family business right out of school, and taken over his father's role in the partnership in the 1820s. Active in the community, the younger Forman was a leading member of groups as diverse as the Horticultural Association and Nova Scotia's Literary and Scientific Society.

When the idea of setting up a new bank made the rounds in the early 1830s, Forman had expressed some interest. He was among those who signed a petition supporting the formation of the Bank of Nova Scotia, but he declined to sign up to buy shares in the enterprise. The cashier's post, though, was another matter. The directors, for their part, were no doubt pleased to place their bank in the hands of someone who shared their place in society. Add the candidate's friendship with Almon, a leading shareholder who was soon to become president, and Forman's hiring was a foregone conclusion.

The new cashier, with an annual salary of £300 – more than double that of the two clerks in his charge – was sent to Saint John, New Brunswick, for a crash course in banking. Forman carried a letter of introduction to the Bank of New Brunswick asking that he be allowed to spend "a few days" observing "the mode of conducting business." This, apparently, was the extent of his formal training. In August 1832, the Bank of Nova Scotia opened its doors for the first time.

The new bank grew rapidly in its early years, adding agencies – the forerunner of branches – in five Nova Scotia communities by 1839. But the initial spurt was followed by decades of slow growth. Dividends paid to shareholders became smaller, and by 1870 the number of agencies had been pared down to three. A series of economic downturns and competition from new banks that sprang up in Halifax in the 1860s partly explained the problem. It was only when serious errors were detected in the books that it became apparent there might be a more insidious reason for the bank's poor performance.

* * *

It fell to Almon to break the news of the embezzlement to the bank's nine-member board of directors at a hastily convened meeting on July 28, 1870. According to the minutes, he announced that Forman "had been guilty of making many fraudulent entries in the books of the Bank, by which he had abstracted a large amount of its funds." Forman had been relieved of his duties and stripped of his keys and account books the night before. Since the cashier's figures could not be trusted, several directors immediately began counting the gold, silver, and banknotes in the vault to find out exactly how much money the bank had on hand.

The next step was facing the shareholders. A brief notice was inserted in Halifax newspapers calling shareholders to a special meeting during the second week of August. No reason was given for the gathering, but word was leaking out that something was seriously wrong. As early as August 2 the bank's agent in Pictou was told to assure customers that their deposits were safe. By the time the shareholders' meeting convened on August 9, rumours had already made their way into the papers that there was a serious shortfall, and Forman was responsible.

The crowd that showed up was so large that the meeting had to be moved from the bank's boardroom to a nearby government building. Although journalists were locked out, there was no shortage of disgruntled shareholders willing to spill the beans afterward. The directors produced a balance sheet showing Forman had helped himself to an astounding $320,000 over the previous twenty-five years. The cashier had already signed over virtually all his property and belongings – houses, building lots, carriages, the family home, even his silverware – to cover part of the loss. Added to the money put up by Forman's bondholders, an estimated $195,000 could be recovered. That still left the bank roughly $125,000 in the hole.

The directors put on a brave face, insisting that the bank was solvent and would have no problem weathering the crisis. But to maintain the confidence of investors and the public alike, a joint committee of shareholders and directors was struck to thoroughly review the bank's books.

There was still the matter of what to do about Forman. One shareholder called for his arrest, which seemed the natural course. But Forman's doctor, who was on hand for the meeting because he held shares in the bank, protested that the cashier was "now so seriously ill that his life might be endangered by such a course." After a brief discussion, the decision on whether to pursue criminal charges was left to the committee set up to sift through the books.

The bank's directors were ridiculed in the Halifax press. How, editorial writers asked, could Forman's massive theft have gone undetected for so long? *The British Colonist* toed the establishment line and suggested the directors had been chastened by the experience; their "negligence or over confidence" would not be repeated. But *The Morning Chronicle* was having none of that. "Mr. Forman's operations were not so cunningly conducted that they could not be easily discovered," a pointed editorial in its August 16 edition observed. "It was well known that he was engaged in heavy speculations, and that his expenditures were far too great for one of his means. Yet the suspicions of those drowsy Directors were not aroused." The president and directors had allowed more than $300,000 "to slip through their fingers, and it is high time they should either resign their positions or be ejected from them."

As for Forman, the *Chronicle* was inclined to think he should face the full weight of the law – social standing, advanced age, and ill health notwithstanding. "His was not the paltry embezzlement of a few dollars, which has before now sent some needy clerk to the penitentiary, but a gigantic theft," the paper pointed out. "The anguish he must suffer is in itself a heavy punishment. Yet while we imprison the urchin who steals an apple we should not pardon the well-informed, able man who steals hundreds of thousands of dollars."

The *Chronicle* acknowledged that it was up to the government and the bank's shareholders to decide whether Forman should be prosecuted. "If they are willing that such a gross swindle should go unpunished by the law, perhaps the rest of the community will be satisfied. Perhaps they will not." One church newspaper took a stronger stance, warning that letting Forman off the hook could prove "a temptation" to others to commit crime. "Justice may, in this instance perhaps, be too much tempered with mercy."

But even as the debate raged over whether to prosecute, Forman was making himself scarce. For a man who was too sick to be arrested, he was well enough to travel. One report said he left Halifax in mid-August on the pretext of visiting relatives in northern Nova Scotia; a few days later he turned up in New York. He eventually moved to London to escape the furor.

The bank sold off Forman's property and possessions at auction in September, including Thorndean, his elegant mansion that still stands on Inglis Street in South End Halifax. That same month Almon stepped down as president, claiming poor eyesight made it impossible for him to sign thousands of new banknotes due to be issued. Few doubted his close association with Forman made it impossible for him to remain in office.

Forman's elegant Halifax mansion, Thorndean on Inglis Street, was sold to recover some of the money he embezzled. (Author photograph)

Meanwhile, the committee set up to review the books was having little success deciphering Forman's handiwork. An independent auditor – William Menzies of the rival Bank of British North America – was hired to establish how much money Forman had skimmed. At the annual shareholders meeting in March 1871, Menzies gave a final figure down to the last penny – $314,967.68. That was slightly below the initial estimate, but still represented about fifteen per cent of the bank's total assets. The sale of Forman's property, on the other hand, was netting less money than hoped. And to make matters worse, the former cashier's bondsmen were disputing how much they should cough up in the wake of the theft. Covering the shortfall ate up an $80,000 reserve fund, all earnings for the first six months of 1870, and close to $28,000 of the bank's capital. Despite the heavy financial burden, a small dividend was paid to mollify the shareholders.

*   *   *

Throughout the embarrassing episode the Bank of Nova Scotia had managed to keep a lid on details of Forman's methods – and the directors' humiliating failure to stop him. But all that changed in the spring of 1872, when the battle with Forman's bondsmen spilled into the courts. Five prominent Halifax businessmen had posted a bond for Forman (a form of insurance, payable if the cashier stole or mishandled money) but only Halifax brewer Alexander Keith, one of the bank's directors, was willing to pay up. The bank sued the bondholders to recover the remaining $22,000 and the whole mess was laid bare in a Halifax courtroom.

Menzies, who was taken on as the new cashier after completing the audit, and Johns, the clerk who first twigged to the theft, took the witness stand to revive the Forman scandal. The new president and three rather sheepish directors also testified. And a letter Forman had written to the bank in late 1870, in which he acknowledged "deficiencies" exceeding $310,000, was read into the record. But the key witness was James Mackintosh, who had been promoted from accountant to deputy cashier after his leading role in uncovering Forman's activities.

Mackintosh revealed that in some cases Forman had swiped tens of thousands of dollars in a single month, including $20,000 stolen soon after he had been bonded. The thefts had begun in 1844 and since the 1850s Forman's personal account had been overdrawn by as much as $47,000. As for the directors, Mackintosh admitted they were oblivious to the overdraft; as accountant, he was required to report overdrawn accounts to only one official, the cashier. That was just one of many examples of the bank's reliance on Forman's honesty rather than a proper system of internal checks and balances. "The cashier could make alterations" in the books, Mackintosh admitted, "as many as he liked."

A jury awarded only $12,000 of the $22,000 sought, a move some interpreted as acknowledging that the directors had been asleep at the switch. Undaunted, the bank went back for more punishment, appealing the verdict. The award was upheld, but not before Chief Justice William Young tore a strip off the bank's directors for their "blind confidence" in Forman.

"Everything was fair on the surface, and everything rotten below," the judge remarked. "The falsifications on the books were endless." In the wake of this "catastrophe," he was happy to report, the province's banks had taken steps to curb the "tremendous and irresponsible power" their cashiers had enjoyed in the past.

* * *

The Bank of Nova Scotia soon rebounded from the Forman affair. With a new cashier and a series of younger, more aggressive presidents, the bank launched a drive to open new agencies and expand business. At the annual shareholders meeting in March 1872, exactly two years after Forman's embezzlement first came to light, the directors proudly declared "that both as respects its finances and credit [the bank] may now be said to have recovered from the effects of the loss by its late Cashier."

Forman was never prosecuted, despite the editorials decrying one form of justice for the rich and another for the poor. There was certainly enough evidence. The bank's decision not to press charges defies an easy explanation, especially when it was willing to wash its dirty linen in public for the sake of trying to squeeze a few thousand dollars from the bondsmen. Forman's ill health and age were undoubtedly taken into account, since it would have been necessary to extradite him from England to face trial. But the deciding factor may have been the directors' reluctance to further punish one of their own. After all, Forman had rubbed shoulders with the cream of Halifax society, even if it turned out that all the while he was betraying everyone around him.

Prosecution soon became a moot point. Forman, stripped of his ill-gotten trappings of wealth at age seventy-six, did not have to endure the stigma of his fall from grace for long. The community leader, trusted employee, and embezzler extraordinaire died in England in August 1871.

5

Three-ring Robbery

It was billed as "The Greatest Show on Earth," and it was coming to Halifax for the first time. Special trains were arranged to bring thousands of spectators into the city on the first three days of August 1876 to see P.T. Barnum's Circus. Advertisements and billboards, using money as a measure of the show's grandeur, boasted that the spectacle was worth $1.5 million, paid $2,000 a day in wages, and filled three "monster" trains.

Patrons were promised "a Noah-like menagerie" of exotic animals, including the only living hippopotamus in North America. Headlining the show's human marvels was Captain Costentenus, a Greek man who had been tattooed from head to foot with 388 images of "birds, beasts and men." Acrobats, trapeze artists, trained elephants, a museum of curiosities and artifacts "from every Clime," and a portrait gallery of "the most distinguished Rulers and Statesmen of the Old and New World" were also featured. Admission to the wondrous show, crammed into three tents set up on the Halifax Common, was fifty cents, a quarter for children under nine, and free to those willing to shell out a princely $1.50 for the nine-hundred-page, illustrated *Life of P.T. Barnum.*

A poster touting the Halifax performances of the "Greatest Show on Earth" – American showman P.T. Barnum's circus and its "Noah-like menagerie" of exotic animals. (Author collection)

Halifax was in the midst of a summer heatwave and turnout was heavy; some 9,000 tickets were sold for just one of the evening performances in a city of 30,000. "There may not be much money in Halifax," noted *The Morning Herald*, "but there will no doubt be enough found to enable every man and his neighbor to be there at some time during the show's stay."

There was no shortage of money at the Bank of Nova Scotia on Hollis Street, a two-storey stone building replete with pillars and gargoyles. And even bank clerks found it hard to resist the lure of the Big Top. On Wednesday morning, August 1, Barnum's performers staged a massive promotional parade through the business district. As it passed the front doors of the bank about half-past eleven, employees abandoned their desks and wickets and joined the throngs of spectators on the sidewalk.

"There was nothing said about going out to see the show among any of the clerks," recalled St. George Twining, who had been a teller at the bank for almost four years. "The movement towards the door was general." All eight employees, including John Nalder, an accountant who was in charge while the cashier was out of town, grabbed their hats and headed outside.

Nalder instructed one of the tellers to lock the door. In his haste to catch a glimpse of the parade, he did not stop to make sure the order was carried out. But Horace Flemming, one of the clerks, locked the door and gave it a rattle to make sure it was secure. They were out of the building for ten minutes, fifteen tops.

Melville Whidden was the first to return. "I found no one there," he swore. "I unlocked the door myself, no one was inside."

Twining returned to his desk and his work. It was another fifteen minutes before he reached for the cashbox he kept in an unlocked drawer. To his shock, it was empty. When he had received it from the safe earlier that morning, it had been stuffed with roughly $17,000 in small bills. More than half was in Bank of Nova Scotia twenty-dollar notes, but there were also bundles of Canadian and Newfoundland currency.

"I first spoke to Mr. Nalder and asked him if he had been meddling with my money," Twining recalled, thinking he was

The Bank of Nova Scotia on Hollis Street in 1869. When the staff rushed outside to watch Barnum's circus parade pass by in the summer of 1876, a pair of enterprising robbers made off with more than $20,000. (William Notman/McCord Museum I-39048.1)

being made the butt of a joke. He also accused Flemming of hiding the cash. But Flemming was scrambling to find about $5,000 that had been in his own desk before the parade passed.

It was no joke. Twining sheepishly entered the office of the bank's president, who had just arrived at work, to break the news: somehow, someone had cleaned out the till to the tune of $22,000.

* * *

Word reached the Halifax police station, just two blocks away at the corner of George Street and Bedford Row, about noon. Sergeants Nicholas Power and Daniel McDonald were dispatched to investigate. Power, a burly Royal Navy veteran who had been with the force for a dozen years, took charge and began interviewing witnesses. The only lead came from Mary Anderson, the wife of one of the bank's messengers, who lived upstairs. About the time the parade passed, she said, someone rapped at the side door, a private entrance serving the upstairs apartments. She answered and was confronted by a stranger who said he had dropped a "valuable paper" through a sidewalk grate that connected to the building's basement. He wanted to go to the cellar to try to retrieve it.

There was nothing strange about the request. Anderson was used to fetching items lost down the grate, but the man pushed past her and said he would get it himself.

"Which way?" he asked as he hurried down the hall.

"Down there," Anderson replied, surprised by the man's boldness. He disappeared into the basement.

Anderson stood at the door and stared down the hall as she waited for the visitor to return. After a few minutes he rushed past her from another direction. He had taken a second stairway leading from the cellar into the bank, then cut through the boardroom to return to the side door. Anderson was again taken by surprise. "He stepped past me so quick that I just asked him if he got the paper; he said 'Yes,' and began to run." He headed south on Hollis Street and disappeared into the crowd. Anderson, who had no idea the bank was empty, thought nothing more of the encounter until the clerks discovered they had been robbed.

The policemen were able to extract only the barest description of the man: short, wore dark clothes and a hat, walked with a limp. It wasn't much to go on, but Power suspected whoever had pulled off the daring heist would be trying to make a getaway. He and McDonald headed for the railway station in the north end of the city.

At Flinn's Hotel, near the depot, they hit pay dirt. Two men, one answering the description, had dropped in to ask where they could hire a wagon. That tip led the policemen to William Hinch, a cabman who lived nearby. Yes, Hinch said, two men, one tall and one short, had tried to hire him about half past twelve. He told them the fare would be five dollars. The shorter man reached into his pocket and pulled out a wad of bills "nearly as thick as my wrist," Hinch said, and peeled off some tens and twenties. He asked his companion if he had a five, and the tall man produced a smaller bundle of bills and found a five.

"I asked them to wait til I got a bite of dinner," Hinch told the policemen. "They said no, they were in a great hurry, they wanted to meet some friends in Bedford," a few miles north of the city. Hinch lined them up with another driver and the pair left. Each man carried a suitcase and the taller one had a small leather satchel tucked under his arm.

Large bundles of bills, suitcases, a short man in a hurry to leave town – Power and McDonald were convinced they were on the right trail.

* * *

Cabman Jonathan Adams had taken the fare. The men asked to stop at an inn on the road to Bedford, and invited Adams in for a beer. The shorter man bought the round. They said they were "circus men" and Adams noted that they left all three pieces of luggage outside in the wagon while they drank, suggesting none of the bags contained anything of value. He left his passengers at the Bedford railway station about two-thirty and returned to Halifax.

Stationmaster George Boggs saw them next, when he looked up from his newspaper. To his disgust, they were sitting in the ladies waiting room, and one was puffing on a cigar. "Gentlemen," he growled after opening his office window, "are you aware you are in the ladies room? Furthermore, you are smoking, which is not allowed."

"Really," said the shorter man. "We'll attend to that." Boggs returned to his desk and resumed reading, but looked up a few minutes later to see the two men were still there.

"When I speak, I expect to be minded ... you will be good enough to walk out." They went outside, but re-entered on the gentlemen's side of the station, rapped on Boggs's window, and asked when the next train would arrive from Halifax. Four o'clock, they were told. They lingered on the platform for a few minutes, then walked over to French's Hotel.

They were sitting down to a meal in the hotel's dining room when sergeants Power and McDonald walked in. There was no one else in the room. "I immediately noticed the short man answered the description given me, and immediately arrested them," Power recalled. "I told them it was for the Bank robbery. They said it was all right or something to that effect."

The men refused to give their names or answer questions. Power searched the shorter man and found a loaded revolver in his pants pocket. He also had twenty dollars in U.S. greenbacks and three dollars in Canadian currency. McDonald searched the other man and found a watch and no more than thirty-five dollars in American bills. There were no thick wads of money like the cabman Hinch had seen. Power retrieved two valises from a room the pair had rented; they contained clothing and a black felt hat.

While Power was out of the room, the short man turned to McDonald and asked: "Were there any more arrested for the affair?"

"What affair?" the policeman asked.

"You must know."

It was a brief exchange, but it implied others were involved. With the stolen money still missing, Power already suspected as much. He caught the train to Truro, the next major town, while McDonald escorted the suspects back to Halifax. Under questioning, the short man said he was C.T. Watson from New York. The taller man gave the name Charles G. Hampton of Springfield, Massachusetts.

That night, Mary Anderson was brought to the police station. She could not identify Watson as the man who entered the bank. But he was wearing a black and white straw hat and a light-coloured overcoat. Next morning she was brought back to take another look. This time Power, who was back from Truro, put the black felt hat from one of the valises on Watson's head. "I would not take an oath positively," she said, "but to the best of my belief that is the man."

The identification was shaky, but it was bolstered by Anderson's servant. Before the circus procession passed the bank, Elizabeth Langille had gone to the side door to take a delivery from a bakery. Just outside, a short man dressed in a dark coat and felt hat was leaning against the building. "Has the show gone by?" she asked the man.

"No, not for an hour," he replied.

Shown Watson at the police station, Langille said she had "no doubt" he was the man. Watson and Hampton were charged with robbery and locked up to await a court hearing.

* * *

The bank clerks were chastised for displaying "the carelessness of children and the curiosity of nursery maids" when news of the robbery broke on August 2. "That grown men, with average intellects, should abandon the care of large sums of money, and leave their desks unlocked, to go out to gaze like raw bumpkins at a passing show," fumed *The Morning Herald*, "is something that excites one's scorn too much to leave room for any pity for the victims of the clever rascality which followed."

But the bank employees were not the only ones who were red-faced. Less than a block away, in the government's treasury office at Province House, a cash box containing about $2,000 had been swiped when employees ducked outside to watch the parade. The box was later found on a waterfront wharf, stripped of everything but a few dollars in change. The bank offered a $2,000 reward for the conviction of the robbers; the government put up $500 more for the arrest of its assailants.

The *Herald* believed The Greatest Show on Earth was partly to blame. "There is no doubt that the circus was followed by some desperate ruffians, and the city is well rid of them," the paper editorialized on August 5. "Thieves hang around Barnum like the cloud of camp followers." The circus did tend to leave empty tills in its wake. The day before the show came to Halifax, the train station in Truro had been robbed of $100 while the circus was performing in the town.

Watson and Hampton seemed to be among those cashing in on the pandemonium that Barnum created. Hampton, condemned as "a noted New York thief" in the press, had served time for robbery in the United States and went by the alias Horace Hampton. Mug shots were becoming a common tool to track criminals but both men refused to pose for photographs that might confirm their identities. Officers hauled them to a commercial studio, but by one report, "they fought and struggled and 'pulled faces'" and ruined every print. Watson later explained away their lack of co-operation by alleging that police had "abused and beaten" them.

Police were searching for at least one other suspect. The small leather satchel they were seen with was missing by the time they were arrested. Had it been passed to an accomplice? Hampton told the police he had taken a room at the International Hotel the night before the robbery. A porter confirmed that he had seen Watson, Hampton, and a third man outside the hotel shortly before the robbery. Further inquiries showed Hampton and a W.H. DeWitt had signed for the room, and Hampton had left a message for a B. Johnston. But these names led nowhere. A week after the robbery, a Halifax detective went to New York to question a man who had been arrested for trying to spend $400 in Bank of Nova Scotia notes. But no charges were laid and the man was released.

There was speculation the robbery had been an inside job. At least one city newspaper put the allegation into print, drawing a stern rebuke from the *Herald*. "Rumours, affecting the honesty of the bank officials, and hints of collusion, are baseless, and are very unkind to those who are already suffering deeply from the consequences of their neglect." The paper that had scolded the clerks now leapt to their defence. "The young men yielded to an impulse to which nine tenths of the population able to walk would have yielded," the *Herald* noted on August 5. "The Bank clerks only did as other mortals did."

But the heist reeked of collusion. If Watson had taken the cash, how did he know he could get inside the bank through the basement? The robber had to duck in, rifle the desks, pocket the money, and duck out, all within a few minutes. The robber had made a beeline for the desks of the only tellers who had large sums of money. It was as if he knew the safe and cashier's room, both containing substantial amounts of cash, were locked. And how could the man seen waiting by the side door have known the bank would be empty, and for how long? The timing seemed too perfect.

The bank's directors huddled in an emergency session within hours of the robbery, but there was no internal investigation and no search of the premises for the money. Heads rolled. St. George Twining, who had lost the bulk of the cash, was fired for carelessness. The other teller who was stung, Horace Flemming, was fired but later rehired. Nalder, the accountant who was in charge on the day of the robbery, was also fired. Within days of the robbery he announced he had received an urgent telegram from his father and had to return to England. He left on the next steamer, his hasty departure adding fuel to the rumours of collusion.

Watson and Hampton were ordered to stand trial in the Supreme Court. Offered a chance to make a statement at the close of a drawn-out preliminary hearing, both men proclaimed their innocence. Watson showed an astonishing grasp of British law by citing legal texts to dispute the magistrate's finding that a trial was warranted. Hampton protested he was "dangerously ill." Their trial was set for November.

* * *

From that point on the case took on the appearance of a circus to rival Barnum's. First, a prosecutor had to be found. The attorney general personally handled Halifax criminal cases, but Otto Weeks, who had held the post for about a year, rarely appeared in court and was neglecting his departmental duties. His problem was the bottle, and his drinking prompted Premier P.C. Hill to remove him from office in late November 1876.

Weeks's absences forced the government to hire lawyers to handle prosecutions. James McDonald, a Pictou Scot with twenty-five years at the bar and a reputation as one of the finest courtroom lawyers of the day, had handled the preliminary hearing for Watson and Hampton. Another lawyer, Samuel Leonard Shannon, was in line to prosecute that month's roster of criminal cases. Shannon was the senior Queen's Counsel in Halifax, but in thirty-seven years of practice he had specialized in real estate and wills, not crime. "In the case of the Bank robbery," Premier Hill noted in a letter to Shannon, "as Mr. McDonald attended to the preliminary investigations, he had better take charge of the indictment." Shannon did most of the talking at trial, but took his cues from McDonald.

Watson and Hampton, meanwhile, had retained the cream of the Halifax defence bar – Robert Motton, whose busy criminal practice kept his name in the papers virtually every day; Robert Weatherbe, talented but quick-tempered, a future chief justice of Nova Scotia; and R.G. Haliburton, son of judge and humorist Thomas Chandler Haliburton.

The defence strategy was simple: throw suspicion on the clerks. Each Bank of Nova Scotia employee who testified was asked point-blank if he knew who had taken the money. Much was made of the accountant's departure for England in the wake of the robbery. And the defence even dredged up the fact that the tellers had been $400 short on an earlier occasion.

Those tactics drew the wrath of the *Herald*. On November 25, beside an account of the day's evidence, the paper published an editorial: "We would be sorry to interfere in cases under the consideration of the court, but we cannot forbear saying that any attempt by the defence to throw the blame of the robbery of the Bank of Nova Scotia on any of the clerks of that institution, will be visited by the indignation of the whole community."

In court later that day, Weatherbe contended the item had been "maliciously inserted for the purpose of creating a prejudice against the prisoners and depriving them of a fair trial." He went further, alleging that Shannon, a shareholder in the newspaper, had inserted the item to bolster the prosecution's case. Shannon, however, assured the court the statements had been published "without my knowledge or consent."

During the debate, a junior lawyer for the prosecution made a crack about a paragraph on the same page of the *Herald* that termed Weatherbe the "'Corny Delany' of Barristers" – an insulting comparison to a well-known, hideous fictional character. Weatherbe saw red. He denounced the lawyer and the newspaper in such "outrageous language" that the judge issued a stern rebuke and ordered Weatherbe to apologize, to the applause of spectators. At least that's how the *Herald*, hardly an objective source, described the incident. Undaunted, the defence sought to have Shannon and the *Herald's* editor cited for contempt of court for trying to influence the jury.

Besides scoring points with the bank clerks, the defence hammered away on the identification of Watson as the man who had entered the bank. After extensive questioning by defence lawyers, Anderson and her servant conceded they would not swear positively that he was the man.

After nine days of evidence and legal wrangling, the jury retired at three o'clock on the afternoon of December 2. At nine, the foreman announced that the jurors were deadlocked. According to press reports, an initial straw vote had been ten for acquittal, two for conviction; those positions remained unchanged through six hours of deliberation. In the wake of the verdict the motion for contempt was abandoned. The *Herald's* criticisms had obviously carried little weight with the jurors.

The defence lawyers applied to have Watson and Hampton released pending a retrial. Several prominent doctors submitted letters certifying that Hampton was suffering from lung problems and should be freed; his prolonged confinement "may perhaps prove fatal," one wrote. He was released on bail and allowed to travel to the States; he did not return for the second trial.

Watson was not so lucky. He remained behind bars in Halifax and was tried again in May 1877. By then the press had lost interest in the case. The *Herald*, which published verbatim accounts of the first trial, almost ignored the sequel. This time the jury retired for three hours and returned a verdict of not guilty. The finding prompted "uproarious applause" from the public galleries, claimed one report, and an elated Watson shook hands with the jurors as they filed out. Free for the first time in nine months, Watson celebrated with dinner at a downtown restaurant and caught a train for the States the following night.

No one was ever convicted of the robbery, and the Bank of Nova Scotia never recovered its money. According to one account of the bank's history, Watson went on to serve time for other thefts and later admitted to a detective that he and Hampton had pulled off the robbery. Stealing $22,000 from a bank in broad daylight when the surrounding streets were crammed with people? It was a feat of daring that would have impressed P.T. Barnum himself.

Part 3

Law of the Sea

A carved wooden likeness of a man's head was salvaged from the *Saladin* after the ship ran aground near Country Harbour on Nova Scotia's Eastern Shore. (Nova Scotia Archives/Harry Piers Collection No. 6158)

6

The Saladin Pirates

The towering masts of a square-rigger slowly emerged from the thick fog as Captain William Cunningham's boat drew near. Heavy surf, whipped by a strong wind, pounded the vessel, which was stuck fast on the shore of a small island. Cunningham spied a handful of crewmen struggling to keep their footing as the deck rolled and breakers burst over the stern.

Cunningham, master of *Billow*, a small coastal schooner bound for Halifax, had taken shelter from the poor weather in Country Harbour on Nova Scotia's Eastern Shore. As his vessel lay at anchor about dawn on May 22, 1844, he was hailed by a group of people on shore, shouting that a large ship had run aground on an island at the mouth of the harbour. Cunningham and his crew manned a longboat to attempt a rescue.

A line was tossed to the stricken ship. Cunningham tied it around his waist and was hauled through the waves to the ship. One crewman begged Cunningham to take command, saying the others had been drinking and could not handle the vessel. All sails were set, and Cunningham feared the wind would shift, pushing the ship away from shore and into deeper water, where it was sure to sink. He ordered the drunken crew to cut the sails loose, to keep the vessel from moving.

Cunningham remained on the ship for a day and a half, working feverishly with the crew to salvage the cargo. And what a valuable cargo it was: several tons of copper; thirteen bars of silver, each weighing 150 pounds; a chest filled with gold coins; and a number of letters containing money. In all, £18,000 worth of goods were saved from the wreck. But the main cargo, barrels of guano – seabird droppings used as fertilizer – was lost. By the time Cunningham left the vessel to the whim of the sea, it was lying on its starboard side, guano washing out of large holes poked in its bottom.

On shore, the authorities were more interested in answers than salvage. Six men were on the ship when it went aground, too few to man such a large vessel. The crew claimed the captain, Alexander McKenzie, had died at sea two months earlier, not long after leaving Valparaiso, Chile, for the British Isles. After that, the mate and two crewmen had fallen from the rigging and were lost overboard.

The story seemed plausible and the crewmen were not detained. But another story soon emerged, a story of treachery, greed, and murder that stands without parallel in Nova Scotia's long history of seafaring. The ship that chance had tossed onto the province's shores had been christened *Saladin*. It was a name that would grow to be synonymous with mutiny and piracy.

* * *

The bloody tale of *Saladin* began in late 1842, when Captain George Fielding sailed from Liverpool, England, as skipper of the barque *Vitula*, bound for Buenos Aires. The son of a British soldier, Fielding was raised in the Gaspé region of Quebec. By the time he reached middle age, he had a reputation as a scoundrel; an acquaintance once expressed surprise that he had somehow managed to escape the gallows. "A most determined villain," noted one writer, a conclusion that Fielding's actions would bear out.

Unable to find any cargo to carry in Argentina, Fielding sailed onward to Valparaiso, on the Pacific coast of South America. Then he hit upon a scheme to turn a fast, if illegal, buck. Heading up the coast to Peru in July 1843, he tried to smuggle a load of guano. But as *Vitula* tied up, Fielding was greeted by fifty Peruvian soldiers intent on seizing the vessel. Fielding distributed weapons to his crew to repulse the boarding party, but the seamen had other plans and fled below deck. Undaunted, Fielding was trying to head back to sea when a soldier shot him in the shoulder.

The ship was seized and taken to Callo, a port near the capital of Lima. Fielding and his crew were thrown in prison, but the crafty skipper had a new plan. His teenaged son, George, helped him to escape. They hid for two days on the waterfront before fleeing on a British steamer bound for Chile. Fielding was now a desperate man. His ship was gone, confiscated by the Peruvians. His only possessions were a few clothes, his navigation instruments and charts, and a Bible. For months he tried in vain to secure passage to England.

Enter Alexander McKenzie, master of the Newcastle-based *Saladin*, a 550-ton barque easily identified by its figurehead – the bust of a Turk complete with turban, earrings, and thick moustache. McKenzie had been at sea twenty years and was a sailor's nightmare. Archibald MacMechan, the great Nova Scotia storyteller, described McKenzie as "an old-fashioned, driving, swearing, drinking, capable son of Neptune." In the words of another writer, "he ruled his crew with a will of iron, bellowed his commands and frequently hastened action with his feet or fists." McKenzie's temperament won obedience but little admiration: *Saladin*'s eleven crewmen called him Sandy behind his back, to show their disrespect.

For reasons known only to McKenzie, he took pity on his stranded countrymen, agreeing to take Fielding and his son to England for free. But *Saladin* had barely cleared Valparaiso's harbour when McKenzie began to regret his uncharacteristic kindness.

"Frequent differences occurred between Capt. McKenzie and Capt. Fielding; the latter in consequence would often refuse to come to [the] table at meals," noted George Jones, the ship's sailmaker. "When Captain McKenzie came on deck, Fielding several times cursed him and used abusive language." As McKenzie told the mate, a man named Bryerly, "it served him right for giving Fielding a passage free." The two men were probably too much alike to get along. There could only be one captain of *Saladin*, and Fielding was determined it would be him.

* * *

After the ship rounded Cape Horn and turned north into the Atlantic, Fielding made his move. He convinced four men to join him in a mutiny. Given McKenzie's rough treatment of the crew, it probably took little persuasion. For good measure, Fielding recruited his henchmen with a combination of threats and promises. Join him, he said, and win a share of the cargo. Side with McKenzie and die.

The chosen four were a motley crew. Jones, the first man approached, was a dark-haired Irishman whose countenance, according to one newsman, was "expressive of suspicion and treachery." He had lost a leg in a fall from a spar and walked on a wooden stump. John Hazelton, twenty-eight, spoke with a nasal twang that made listeners think he was from the Southern States, but he was believed to be a Nova Scotian. William Travaskiss, short and stout, was a twenty-three-year-old Londoner who went by the alias Johnston. He had joined *Saladin* in Chile, claiming he'd been discharged from an American warship. Charles Gustavus Anderson, a Swede who spoke broken English, was the son of a shipbuilder. Although only nineteen, he was Fielding's most willing accomplice. When Fielding made his pitch, Anderson is purported to have replied: "By God, I'll take a knife and cut [McKenzie's] throat. He shall no more strike me away from the helm."

Jones soon had second thoughts and tried to warn McKenzie that Fielding planned to kill him, but McKenzie cut him off. "You damned Irishman, I want to hear nothing," he snapped. The deed was to be done on the night of April 13 – appropriately, a Friday – when Anderson, Johnston, and Hazelton were on watch. But Jones remained below deck, unwilling to join the mutineers. The attack was put on hold and the next morning Fielding had some words of wisdom for Jones: "There is no use making a fool of yourself; if you go back your life is no more."

Unable to warn McKenzie or to back out, Jones showed up the following night. The mutineers armed themselves with hammers, axes, and other tools the ship's carpenter had left in one of the lifeboats. The mate, Bryerly, who was complaining of sickness, was lying on the roof of a cabin. He was quickly dispatched with an axe and his body was thrown overboard without a sound.

McKenzie would be next, Fielding decided. He sent Anderson and Hazelton to the captain's cabin, but they aborted their mission, fearing McKenzie's dog would bark and awaken the rest of the crew. Fielding then chose the carpenter as the next to die. As three men waited in ambush around the hatch, they called the carpenter on deck and struck him down. Thinking him dead, they threw him over the side, but the doomed man began to shout after hitting the water.

Fielding saw his chance. "Man overboard!" he shouted. Just as he expected, McKenzie, clutching a Bible he had been reading, scrambled from his cabin and ordered the helmsman to come about. As he emerged on deck, Anderson struck him a glancing blow with an axe. McKenzie grabbed Anderson but was tackled from behind by Jones. As McKenzie wrestled with the two crewmen, he looked up and saw Fielding brandishing an axe. "Damn you, I will give it to you," Fielding yelled, killing McKenzie with two blows. Fielding hauled the body to the side, struck it a third time for good measure, and threw it overboard.

"The vessel is now our own," Fielding declared, and he invited his followers below for a drink. Fortified with liquor, they went back on deck and discussed how to rid the ship of the remaining five crewmen. It was nearing dawn, so someone called for the morning watch to come on deck. Jem Allen, roused from sleep, walked over to the rail and scanned the ocean. Anderson quietly stole up from behind and knocked him overboard with one swipe of his axe. Thomas Moffat and Sam Collins came up next, and Moffat innocently sat on a spar between Johnston and Hazelton. In a flash his shipmates produced their weapons and Moffat fell to the deck in a pool of blood. At almost the same instant, Anderson murdered Collins with a hammer. Two more bodies were tossed into the sea.

Six men dead, two to go. But the mutineers had a change of heart and decided they had done enough killing. When William Carr, the cook and a middle-aged father of two, came on deck in the morning, he spotted the blood where Moffat had been killed and walked to the stern to find out what had happened. Gathered around the ship's wheel, he found Fielding, Anderson, Johnston, Jones, and Hazelton. At their feet were axes, hammers, and other tools, covered in blood.

"What is the matter?" was the best Carr could say in his confusion.

"Come up, we will not harm you," said Fielding. "I am commander of this vessel now. The master and crew have gone away and left us."

Carr looked around and protested that all the lifeboats were in their places. "It is impossible," he stammered. But the truth was slowly sinking in.

"We have finished Sandy," Fielding continued. "We shall have no more cursing and swearing now. We have finished the carpenter, mate, and Jemmy, Moffat, and Sam. Will you join us?"

"I suppose if I do not join you, I must go the same road as the rest?" Carr knew the answer. He chose to live.

Cabin boy John Galloway, the teenaged son of a Scottish bookseller, was then told to join them on the deck. Fielding announced that the captain and the rest of the crew were dead. "I thought they were making sport of me," he recalled, but it was no joke. He too chose to remain with the living.

Fielding set a new course northward, in the direction of the Gaspé and Newfoundland – areas he knew well. His plan was to leave *Saladin* in a secluded cove and return with a new ship to remove the copper, silver bars and other valuables. Carr was ordered to cook breakfast and Fielding and his cohorts retired to the main cabin and broke into the ship's supply of liquor. "They then began to brag which was the best murderer, laughing and jesting with each other," Galloway recalled. On Fielding's instructions they rifled the captain's desk in search of money, then broke into the mail being carried to England. Banknotes intended to cover postage were removed and the letters burnt. The dead men's clothing was brought into the cabin and divvied up.

Fielding had two more requests of his followers. He ordered all weapons thrown overboard, "because we might get jealous of one another," as Johnston put it. Then Fielding pulled out a Bible. Each man in turn took it in hand and swore to be "loyal and brotherly" to the others. But the strange oath of allegiance would carry little weight among men bound together only by greed and mutual distrust.

The crew quickly discovered there was good reason to be suspicious of their new commander. Even as he swore on the Bible, Fielding was plotting his next move. Still fuming because Carr and Galloway had been spared, he let it be known he wanted them dead before the ship reached land. Two or three days after the murders, Hazelton discovered a set of pistols in the main cabin. The crew confronted Fielding, who denied he had hidden them there. But Galloway and Anderson revealed that Fielding had approached each of them with a scheme to kill Johnston, Carr, and Jones and increase the survivors' share of the loot.

With that, the men turned on Fielding, binding his hands and feet. A search below deck uncovered a carving knife, gunpowder, ammunition, and jugs of brandy that tasted of poison. Through the night the men argued over what to do. All the while Fielding cursed at them, accusing them of having plotted to kill him all along. He "said we wished to take his life, that we were afraid of him," said Carr.

The next morning Fielding's legs were untied and he was brought on deck. Who decided to impose the death sentence was never made clear. Carr and Galloway claimed that the other four – Jones, Johnston, Hazelton, and Anderson – compelled them to act. Carr claimed they were ordered to "heave Fielding overboard, as we had not committed any other crime, and we should do that to be as bad as them." Johnston told the same story, but Jones and Hazelton insisted that drowning Fielding was Carr's idea. "Carr said he never would sleep happy till Fielding was overboard," according to Hazelton.

Fielding, realizing the men meant business, begged Galloway to free his hands. The cabin boy refused. Jones and Carr took him to the rail and threw him overboard. Since all feared Fielding's son would turn them in once they reached land, Carr and Galloway seized the boy. He clung desperately to Galloway's sleeve but was shaken off and slipped beneath the waves.

The remaining six had their hands full manning the ship, a challenge compounded by frequent bouts of drinking. To prevent the ship from being recognized, the figurehead was painted white and a board was nailed over the name on the stern. "We all took an oath never to divulge what had taken place on board the *Saladin*," said Carr. Galloway, the best-educated of the lot, assumed the role of navigator, and headed for the Gulf of St. Lawrence. There, the men agreed, they would divide up the money, scuttle the ship, and head for shore in a lifeboat. But their plan was dashed when they ran aground near Country Harbour.

* * *

Saladin's crewmen dispersed after the rescue, in search of work on other vessels. But questions arose as the authorities began looking through items salvaged from the ship. Some of the clothing was too small for a man and some charts bore the name of Capt. George Fielding. The crew was arrested within twenty miles of Country Harbour and ferried to Halifax in a naval vessel. The six men arrived in late May 1844, in leg irons and under heavy military guard.

They were brought before a judge and, as before, said the captain had died at sea and the other crewmen had been lost overboard. Asked about the charts, they explained that Fielding died before the voyage and his personal effects were being taken to relatives in Britain. But documents found on board showed Fielding sold some of his belongings the day before *Saladin* left Chile. As the prosecutor, Attorney General James W. Johnston, pointed out later, "there were, upon close inspection, local discrepancies, and contradictions in matters of detail" in the stories told by the crewmen. One newspaper, the *Halifax Journal*, told its readers that "there is great reason to fear that piracy, if not worse, has been committed."

The crew was locked up until more information could be obtained from Chile, a process that would take months. But the inquiries proved unnecessary. On June 8 Carr and Galloway sent for Michael Tobin, a politician who was investigating the wreck as agent for the vessel's insurer, Lloyds of London. Tobin, accompanied by the attorney general and the sheriff, went to the prison and took written statements describing the bloody events on *Saladin*.

Armed with the new evidence, Tobin visited Hazelton, who refused to co-operate. But over the next few days Johnston, Jones, and Anderson signed confessions. Hazelton, approached a second time, followed suit. Charges of murder and piracy were laid against Jones, Johnston, Hazelton, and Anderson. Carr and Galloway were to be tried separately for the murders of Fielding and his son.

"Commerce is extending her relations into every portion of the globe, and every sea is whitening with her sails," Attorney General Johnston said, his rich voice echoing through the packed galleries of Halifax's Supreme Court chamber. "It is our duty to throw the protection of the law around those who go down to the sea in ships – it is that alone which can give security to the mariner, and guard the interests of the whole civilized world."

It was a tall order for the court convened in July 1844 to try the first four defendants, but Johnston was confident. "One tenth of what these men did would constitute the crime of Piracy," he maintained. As he concluded his opening remarks, Johnston admitted that the prosecution's evidence rested almost entirely on the confessions of those on trial. "Each tried to extenuate and soften his own share in the transaction," he noted, but "there would be found a general agreement running through the whole."

The "general agreement" was that eight men had been murdered, but the confessions raised questions about who killed whom. Anderson, Jones, and Hazelton said Johnston started the ball rolling by murdering the mate; Johnston insisted he was in another part of the ship at the time. Johnston also denied their assertions that he had taken part in the killing of crewman Moffat.

As the attorney general pointed out, each man tried to distance himself from the murders. Anderson freely admitted killing the ship's carpenter and two of the crewmen, but claimed he acted out of fear for his life. "They told me on the night of the mutiny, that if I did not help them, they would kill me." Hazelton said he axed Moffat because "I was afraid if I did not strike, Johnston would strike me." All agreed that Jones had been at the wheel and killed no one, but he had to explain why he had held McKenzie as Fielding hacked him to death with an axe. Fielding, Jones said, had threatened "if you don't lay hold of him, I will give you a clout that will kill you."

The confessions of Carr and Galloway were of no help in sorting out the guilty from those compelled to act; both men had been asleep below when the killings occurred. And the others did their best to spread the guilt around. Jones and Hazelton said murdering Fielding was Carr's idea. The same two said Galloway laughed when told McKenzie was dead and expressed regret he had not had a chance to take "a cut at Sandy."

Defence lawyer William Young, a short, stout man with a full beard, asked few questions and called no evidence. In his closing address, he stressed that Fielding had been the instigator of the crime. Evidence the four had killed out of fear for their own lives, he said, "was the only ground of hope for, if not acquittal, at least a recommendation of mercy."

Chief Justice Brenton Halliburton, the presiding judge, rejected this weak defence. "I can find here no justification, and I regret to add, no ground of excuse for the offence." There had been ample opportunity for the four men to warn the others, he said, and join them to foil Fielding's plot.

The jury retired for a scant fifteen minutes before declaring all four men guilty. Halliburton took the same hard line when Carr and Galloway stood trial the next day for the murders of Fielding and his son. Nevertheless, both men were acquitted and set free. On Saturday, July 20, the court passed the death sentence on Jones, Anderson, Johnston, and Hazelton.

*   *   *

The final scenes in the *Saladin* saga were enacted on the morning of July 30 on a hill on Halifax's South Common, now the site of the Victoria General Hospital. Thousands gathered for the show; one man, Willam Snyder, walked more than fifty miles from Conquerall Bank, near Bridgewater, to witness the hangings. Soldiers of the 52nd Regiment, bayonets fixed, surrounded the scaffold to keep the throng at a distance.

P.H. Lenoir was just ten years old when her father took her to view the spectacle. "The big open space was crowded with people," she would recall ninety years later, as a procession of soldiers and carriages approached along Tower Road. "The four condemned men stepped out of the prison wagon. ... They were dressed in

HALIFAX.

EXECUTION OF HAZLETON, JOHNSTON, ANDERSON, AND JONES, THE PIRATES OF THE SALADIN.

The execution of the above condemned prisoners took place on Tuesday last.

The prisoners left the penitentiary at ten o'clock, in the waggons of the prison, headed by a corps of the grenadiers, with fixed bayonets, and by the Sheriff in his gig, and followed by an escort of soldiers. The prisoners were attended by their religious advisers—Hazleton and Jones by the Revd. Fathers O'Brien, Connolly, and Quinan, and Anderson and Johnston by the Rev. W. Cogswell.

The scaffold was erected on a rising ground, at the lower side of the Common, and the prisoners ascended the steps with a firm step. Their demeanor was that of contrition. The preliminaries were arranged under the direction of the Sheriff, to whom the highest credit is due for the quiet, orderly, and expeditious manner in which every part of the ceremony was conducted.

It was an awful sight! Within the view of the scaffold, these unhappy men could see the blue waters stretching far into that ocean which they had stained with blood, while around them on every side were the dread implements of death—the sable executioner—the bolts of the fatal drop—the coffins beneath the scaffold—

A report on the execution of the four *Saladin* pirates, published in the Pictou-based *Eastern Chronicle* in 1844. (Author collection) black with white shirts. Each man had a coil of rope round his arm, the other end of which was knotted around his neck."

The prisoners, accompanied by clergymen, mounted the gallows. Below lay four coffins. The men shook hands and Jones spoke briefly, telling the crowd he was sorry for what he had done and asking for a pardon from God. Lenoir was too far away to hear Jones's words. "White hoods were pulled over their faces," she wrote in a memoir. "The next moment four bodies shot into the air and continued to dangle there. Never have I forgotten the sight."

7

The Skipper's Good Name

The piece of short fiction featured in the October 1946 issue of *Cosmopolitan* would catch the eye of any Nova Scotian. "The Miracle of Sable Island" was a tale about the rescue of starving ponies from the barren island off the Nova Scotia coast. The magazine promised readers they would find it "unforgettable."

The author was Edmund Gilligan, a rotund, forty-six-year-old former newspaperman. He had served as a sailor during the First World War and after working for dailies in Boston and New York, and *Time* and *Fortune* magazines, he had abandoned journalism to pump out short stories and novels about the sea.

"The Miracle of Sable Island" was not distinguished by its attention to detail – the main character, an elderly Lunenburg sea captain, spoke more like a pirate than a South Shore fisherman. But the magazine raised the ire of one famous Nova Scotian seafarer over something more serious than an accent. *Cosmopolitan*'s editors had written a blurb introducing the story and its writer, and that's what caused all the fuss.

"Gilligan can't understand why more writers don't turn to the North Atlantic coast country in their search for fiction material," they wrote. "The seafolk of Nova Scotia with their unchanging traditions, their strong religious beliefs and their rugged physical life fascinate him."

Those generalizations were enough to make any Nova Scotian bristle, but the editors were more specific: "He tells, for example, of visiting Lunenburg recently and inquiring about a well-known sea captain. 'He's delivering milk,' said a fisherman with scorn and contempt. 'He's lost his ship and he lives ashore delivering milk, and that's what he deserves. None of us will have anything to do with him.' Why, Gilligan asked, did this misfortune come upon the captain. 'Why?' said the fisherman with rising indignation. 'For a very good reason. Because he cursed the Lord, that's why!'"

"It seems," the editor's note continued, "that the captain took his schooner, a famous racing ship, on tour through the Great Lakes. In Chicago a girl sight-seer happened to touch the schooner's wheel with her hand, and the captain was so enraged at this violation that he called a curse upon God for permitting it. The people of Lunenburg will never forgive him. They think it only just that he is no longer a prosperous sea captain."

The disgraced sea captain was not named, but his identity was obvious. It could be none other than Angus Walters, who had skippered *Bluenose* to victory over American rivals in the international fishermen's races of the 1920s and 1930s. He had sailed the famous schooner on the Great Lakes to the Chicago World's Fair in 1933, and he was the only retired Lunenburg sea captain involved in the dairy business – as the owner of a dairy, not as a deliveryman. And as for losing his vessel, Walters had sold *Bluenose* in 1942 after an unsuccessful public appeal for money to preserve the schooner.

His reaction to the article can best be gauged from a biography written less than a decade later. "He was the first to admit that there had been occasions when he used language foreign to drawing-room conversation," author G.J. Gillespie noted, "but when it came to cursing the Lord that was a different matter."

Captain Angus Walters on board the *Bluenose* with the North Atlantic Fishermen's International Trophy after winning the 1921 racing series. (W.R. MacAskill/Nova Scotia Archives No. 1987-453/261)

After reading the *Cosmopolitan* item, Walters consulted a lawyer. He sued the magazine for libel, for sullying his reputation as a skilled and respected sailor. Walters had soundly thrashed the Americans on the water; he was coming out of retirement to take them on one more time, in court.

* * *

The names Angus Walters and *Bluenose* are inseparable. He was the only man to skipper the sleek schooner. Her moments of glory were his moments of glory. And when captain and vessel headed off to race America's best, they carried with them the burden of defending Nova Scotia's long seafaring tradition.

Bluenose was built specifically to restore the province's pride in that legacy – a legacy tarnished in the fall of 1920, in the first race for the North Atlantic Fishermen's International Trophy. William H. Dennis, publisher of *The Halifax Herald*, and a group of Halifax businessmen had sponsored the competition as an alternative to the America's Cup, which had been hijacked by wealthy yachtsmen. These races would feature Canadian and American schooners – real sailing vessels manned by men who had earned their sea legs fishing cod on the Grand Banks.

In the first series of races for the fishermen's cup, the Nova Scotia representative, *Delawana*, lost badly to *Esperanto* out of Gloucester, Massachusetts. Humiliated by the defeat, the Halifax backers of the racing series resolved to win back the trophy for Nova Scotia. An amateur naval architect, William J. Roué, was retained to design a schooner to carry Nova Scotia's colours in the next round of races. On March 26, 1921, the 143-foot *Bluenose* slipped down the ways of the Smith & Rhuland shipyard in Lunenburg, ready for battle.

Walters, a thirty-nine-year-old Lunenburg fishing captain, was chosen to command the challenger. "Angus Walters and *Bluenose* were something out of the ordinary: a remarkable marriage of vessel and master," Nova Scotia writer Silver Donald Cameron noted in a 1984 book chronicling their exploits. The son of a sea captain, Walters had gone to sea at thirteen as a deckhand and was skipper of his own schooner by age twenty-four. He held the record for the largest single catch landed by a Nova Scotia vessel, and was known as a wily, hard-driving master whose sailing skill had more than once saved vessel and crew from a watery grave.

And when it came to racing other vessels into port, Walters was a born competitor. "He was a genius where sailing was concerned," recalled Paul Crouse, a *Bluenose* crewman in the 1930s. Another former crewman put it more bluntly: "Angus was a bugger to carry sail." Walters supervised construction of *Bluenose*, and liked what he saw. "I knew from the beginning she was a winner," he recalled. "I just figured she was a little faster than their best." They, of course, were the Americans. "In those days the Americans were the cock of the walk in everything they did," he noted with disdain. In *Bluenose*, he saw a way to cut them down to size.

Bluenose recaptured the International Fishermen's Trophy in the fall of 1921, thrashing the Gloucester schooner *Elsie*. The trophy never left Nova Scotia again. *Bluenose* successfully defended the title in 1922 and 1923, but the races were becoming acrimonious. *Bluenose* retained the trophy in 1923 only after Walters quit the series in a huff (he had lost one leg of the race on a technicality) and the American challenger refused to take the title by default.

It was eight years before racing resumed. In the meantime, despite the legend that *Bluenose* was never beaten, the vessel lost a 1930 race for the Lipton Cup to the Boston schooner *Gertrude L. Thebaud*. But, in races for the International Fishermen's Trophy the following year, 1931, and in 1938, Walters and *Bluenose* redeemed themselves, defeating *Thebaud* both times.

The 1938 series was *Bluenose's* last hurrah. Walters, who owned the bulk of the shares in the schooner, used it to fish on the Banks and to haul freight. The era of the working sailing vessel had passed, and Walters reluctantly retired from the sea. In 1940 he opened a dairy in Lunenburg, but refused to give up on his beloved vessel. When the sheriff seized the schooner to repay a debt owing on its diesel engines, Walters cashed in his life insurance policy and scraped up $7,000 to keep it off the auction block. He mounted a drive to preserve *Bluenose* as a piece of Nova Scotia history, but there was little public interest at a time when war raged around the globe. In 1942 he sold the vessel to the West Indies Trading Company, to carry freight between islands in the Caribbean.

"There was a lump in my throat," Walters recalled of the day he cast off *Bluenose's* lines for the last time. "I knew it was goodbye, and she was like part of me. To tell the goddamn truth, when I walked home, I felt like I was coming out of the cemetery."

Four years later, on the evening of January 29, 1946, someone tracked down Walters at the Lunenburg curling rink with bad news. *Bluenose* had struck a reef off Haiti and sunk. Walters, the man who epitomized the age of wooden ships and iron men, wept.

* * *

Just nine months after *Bluenose* was lost, *Cosmopolitan* served up another shock for Walters. Established in 1886, *Hearst's International Combined with Cosmopolitan*, to give the magazine's full title, was part of the empire built by newspaper magnate William Randolph Hearst. Based in New York, the magazine circulated worldwide and sold well in the Maritime Provinces. More than 2,300 copies of the October 1946 issue, at thirty-five cents a copy, were sold on Nova Scotia newsstands, and several hundred people in the Atlantic region shelled out four dollars a year to subscribe.

Articles in the issue that included "The Miracle of Sable Island" were a combination of short fiction, profiles of celebrities such as Broadway star Fannie Brice, photo features, and self-help items. A feature on war-torn Germany was contributed by a youthful GI reporter named Andy Rooney, who went on to be a regular on the television news magazine *60 Minutes*. The issue's 224 pages were crammed with advertisements for clothes, liquor, personal care products, and cars. An ad for Studebaker, strutting the motto "First by far with a postwar car," depicted the sleek, "daringly different" 1947 models.

To Walters, the only thing that mattered was the paragraph on page four about the Lunenburg sea captain. He retained Halifax lawyer Charles B. Smith, who demanded satisfaction. *Cosmopolitan's* lawyers responded in May 1947 with an offer: "We would publish a complete retraction along the lines that Capt. Walters was not the one referred to in our former publication, together with some favorable statement about his success at defeating the United States a number of times in sailing races." The magazine was also willing to pay $750 to compensate Walters and cover his legal expenses.

The proposal would have only added insult to injury, tying Walters' name to the description of a disgraced sea captain for readers who had not already made the connection. Walters revealed what he thought of the $750 payment at the end of July, when his lawyer filed a libel suit with the Nova Scotia Supreme Court, seeking damages totalling $15,000. The lawsuit claimed Walters had been "held up to ridicule and contempt." The article

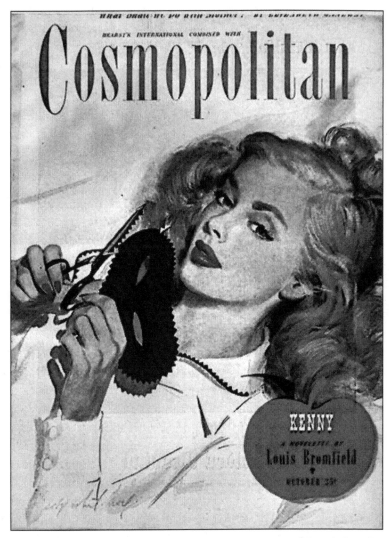

The October 1946 issue of *Cosmopolitan* magazine claimed that the former captain of "a famous racing ship" was a pariah in Lunenburg because he had "cursed the Lord." (Author collection)

falsely stated that he was scorned by the people of Lunenburg, had been "reduced to delivering milk for a living," and was "guilty of blasphemy." And he had been libelled not only in Nova Scotia, but across Canada and in the United States and Britain, where he was "well-known by reason of his former activities as master of the famous racing schooner *Bluenose*."

The Hearst publishing empire was hardly shaken to its foundations. *Cosmopolitan's* lawyers gave Smith the run-around and ignored his phone calls when he was in New York on other business. In September, working through lawyers in Halifax, the magazine applied to have the lawsuit thrown out, claiming the Nova Scotia courts lacked jurisdiction. Hearst argued that the magazine was distributed in Nova Scotia by subsidiary companies and an independent wholesale news dealer, H.H. Marshall Ltd. Following that logic, Hearst Magazines Inc., the defendant named in the lawsuit, was not responsible for publishing the offensive article in the province.

But Justice John Doull rejected the magazine's bid to derail the lawsuit. Even if he accepted the argument that others had spread the alleged libel, the Supreme Court judge noted in a ruling handed down in September 1947, Hearst was still responsible for copies mailed to subscribers. And Nova Scotia was the proper venue for resolving the suit, he noted. "In all its elements this seems to be a Nova Scotia case." Doull went on to make two comments that bolstered Walters' cause. The passages that had raised the sea captain's ire were, on their face, libellous. And, he added, "I am probably not going very far when I say that a great many people who would read the words in Nova Scotia would consider that the reference" was to Walters.

Hearst Magazines took no further action. Faced with the probability that the suit would succeed, based on one judge's assessment at least, the company did not file a defence. Walters won by default. On the last day of October, the Supreme Court issued a judgment against Hearst, and a hearing was set for December 12 to determine how much Walters was entitled to receive in damages.

Smith called three witnesses. Robert J. Rankin, managing editor of *The Halifax Herald*, testified there was "no doubt" in his mind that most Nova Scotians would have thought Walters was the unidentified captain referred to in *Cosmopolitan*. An official of H.H. Marshall Ltd. provided circulation figures for the magazine in the Maritimes.

Then Walters took the stand. Smith led his client through a thumbnail sketch of his exploits as *Bluenose* captain, including the 1933 Great Lakes tour and a 1935 audience with King George V. Then he turned to the magazine's allegations. Walters denied making a scene because a woman touched *Bluenose*'s wheel in Chicago. "I won't be exaggerating to say that the *Bluenose* was steered more by the passengers, more so by the female sex than the male sex, while we were on Lake Michigan."

Walters, now sixty-six, described his decision to sell *Bluenose* (he had not "lost" the vessel), retire from the sea, and open a dairy. "I couldn't attempt the dairy business and look after the vessel too. It was too much for me."

"Previous to reading this article, had anybody informed you that you were held up to scorn and contempt in the Town of Lunenburg?" the lawyer asked.

"What would I do with the milk? The milk wouldn't be much good to me if nobody in Lunenburg had anything to do with me."

"Is there any truth in the allegation you cursed the Lord?"

"I was no saint when I went fishing," Walters admitted. "Not one today – but I don't think I would stoop so low as to curse the Lord for something he had nothing to do with."

* * *

The task of assessing damages fell to the silver-haired chief justice, Joseph Chisholm, a student of Nova Scotia history who had been top judge for fifteen years. "A kindly soul," recalled one lawyer, "his reasoned application of the law won him the love and respect, not only of the Bar, but of the entire Halifax community."

But in a ruling delivered four days before Christmas, 1947, Chisholm had few kind words for *Cosmopolitan*. The statements about Walters were "malicious" and "grossly false," he said, and the magazine had made no effort to ascertain whether they were correct. The judge angrily attacked *Cosmopolitan*'s offer to settle the case for $750 and a retraction. "To say that the plaintiff was not the party referred to," he said, "would only be to add another falsehood to those already published." Despite the harsh words, Chisholm gave Walters only a fraction of the $15,000 sought in the lawsuit. Damages were set at $3,500.

Walters' reaction to the outcome of the case is unknown. The lawsuit and the ruling against *Cosmopolitan* were covered in detail in the Halifax press, helping to restore any harm done to his image. When he was well into his seventies Walters was still puttering around his dairy, and he came out of retirement in 1957 to pilot a small government vessel from Lunenburg to Lake Superior. He sailed on the maiden voyage in 1963 of *Bluenose II*, the replica he had wanted built ever since the original sank. He died August 12, 1968, his reputation intact, his place in history secure.

8

Mutiny on the Zero

The mysterious square-rigger was under sail and only a quarter mile from shore, but James Baker could see no sign of the crew. He pulled his fishing boat alongside and clambered aboard, but all he found was a dog. It was the morning of September 11, 1865, and the LaHave Islands fisherman had stumbled onto a crime scene.

The wheel had been tied off with rope, to keep the vessel on course until it sank or ran aground. The cabin doors were ajar and, below deck, Baker recalled, "everything was upside down and in confusion." Damage to the hull suggested someone had tried to scuttle the vessel. Planks near the waterline had been chopped with an axe, allowing about two feet of water to seep into the hold. And black paint had been used to hide the vessel's name, leaving only the letter R.

Baker and his companions, eager to claim salvage on the 200-ton ship and its cargo of coal, sailed it into LaHave Harbour on Nova Scotia's South Shore. Other fishermen fanned out in search of the crew. They spotted a small boat on a beach and found three men who said they were from *Zero*, which had sprung a leak while carrying coal from Cape Breton Island to New York.

The mate, John C. Douglas, did all the talking. The cook, Henry Dowcey, and the cabin boy, Frank Howard Stockwell, nodded in agreement as Douglas explained that the captain, Colin C. Benson, had fallen overboard and drowned a few nights earlier. When the crew abandoned *Zero*, it had six feet of water in the hold and was sinking fast, Douglas claimed. They had come ashore and two other crewmen, Germans named Charles Marlbey and William Lambruert, had gone off on their own.

The fishermen were suspicious. *Zero* remained afloat, they reported, and had little water in its hold. Asked about the attempted scuttling, Douglas offered the dubious suggestion that another vessel must have overtaken the abandoned *Zero*, and its crew had painted out the name and tried to sink it.

It was obvious the mate was lying about why the vessel had been abandoned, and perhaps about how the captain died as well. The fishermen ferried the trio to the mainland, where the authorities could try to find out why. Those inquiries would expose a shocking tale of high-seas treachery and murder – and launch the courtroom career of a brilliant young Halifax lawyer destined to become prime minister of Canada.

* * *

The mate, cook, and cabin boy were brought before a magistrate the following day. When all three insisted the captain had died accidentally, they were released. But Attorney General William A. Henry, who was not convinced they were telling the truth, ordered Sergeant Lewis Hutt of the Halifax police to investigate.

Hutt rounded up Douglas and found Stockwell in Windsor, on the other side of the province. Dowcey, Lambruert, and Marlbey were arrested in Liverpool, a port just thirty miles from where *Zero* was discovered. Hutt was still in Liverpool with his prisoners when he was handed a telegram reporting that Douglas and Stockwell had changed their stories. Dowcey, they now said, had murdered the captain and thrown his body into the sea. The

TRAGEDY AT SEA.

The Halifax *Morning Chronicle* says :—Our readers are already familiar with the fact that about ten days ago the brig Zero, built in this province, but now owned in New York, was found by some fishermen abandoned off the harbour of Le Have, Lunenburg county, and subsequently brought into this port. Upon the brig being boarded by the sailors, it was found that she was plentifully supplied with stores and all the necessary appliances for navigating her to her destination. Upon further investigation it was discovered that an attempt had been made to scuttle her by cutting a hole in each side, from the exterior just at the water line, but the perforation was not complete. It was also observed that the name on the stern had been obliterated with black paint. The sailors took the vessel into Le Have, and reported these circumstances to the authorities. Suspicion was at once awakened that all was not right, and the circumstances of the case were telegraphed to the Provincial Government. In the meantime the mate of the Zero, the

"Suspicion was at once awakened that all was not right," Halifax's *Morning Chronicle* reported after the discovery of the abandoned brig *Zero* near LaHave, Lunenburg County. (Author collection)

sergeant confronted Dowcey with the news. "The mate will get clear because he has turned Queen's evidence," the cook said angrily. It would be every man for himself.

Dowcey and the two Germans were shipped to Halifax. After appearing before a Halifax magistrate on October 10, Dowcey, Douglas, and Lambruert were ordered to stand trial for the murder of Benson. "From such hints as transpire from those who have the best means now of knowing facts," reported the *Unionist*, a Halifax newspaper, "we are apt to think that the catalogue of crime has rarely produced a more cruel, brutal murder."

The 1865 trial of three crewmen accused of murdering Colin Benson, the captain of the *Zero*, was held in Halifax's newly opened courthouse on Spring Garden Road. (William Notman/McCord Museum I-39054.1)

The trial opened on November 9, 1865, in Halifax's newly built sandstone courthouse on Spring Garden Road. After the presiding judge, Chief Justice William Young, turned down a defence application for the three men to be tried separately, twelve jurors were selected and the Crown opened its case.

Prosecutor Jonathan McCully's star witness was Stockwell, the cabin boy, the son of a Springfield, Massachusetts, Baptist minister who had defied his parents and run away to sea. Although only fifteen, he struck the reporter for Halifax's *Evening Express* as "very intelligent ... everyone who heard him being impressed with the conviction that he was telling the truth."

Stockwell gave a chilling account of Benson's murder. The youth said he had joined *Zero* in New York, as had the cook, Dowcey. Douglas was already on board as mate. When the vessel took on its cargo of Nova Scotia coal, Marlbey and Lambruert joined the crew. Other than a minor dispute between the captain and the Germans over wages, it was a routine voyage until Sunday morning, September 10.

Benson turned in about four in the morning, leaving Lambruert at the wheel. Stockwell awoke at dawn and roused Dowcey, who began preparing the morning meal. After he heard "an unusual noise" coming from the captain's cabin, the cook yelled his name and told him to summon Lambruert. Stockwell went on deck and relieved Lambruert at the wheel. When the German returned, he was wringing his hands. "The cook," he exclaimed, "has killed the captain."

Stockwell headed below and found the rest of the crew in the quarters they shared. Douglas was casually smoking a pipe. "Frank, go to the captain's cabin and help the cook," Douglas told Stockwell, who noted there were tears in the mate's eyes. Stockwell, who by now realized the captain was dead, said he would rather jump overboard. Douglas repeated the order to Marlbey and Lambruert. They complied.

Stockwell watched as Dowcey and Lambruert carried Benson on deck, wrapped in a sheet. One side of his head was bloody and smashed in – the result of four blows inflicted with an iron bar as he slept – but he was still alive.

"Don't, man, and I will go anywhere with you," Benson pleaded as he was tossed into the sea. Stockwell went to the rail. The captain continued to struggle as he sank beneath the calm sea.

The five crewmen assembled in their quarters. Douglas and Lambruert were crying, by Stockwell's account; Dowcey was "half laughing and half crying." Douglas told Dowcey to wash his bloody hands. "God, that's nothing," the cook replied, wiping his hands on his shirt. Dowcey retrieved the paperwork for the voyage from the captain's cabin and handed the documents to Douglas. "We can't do as we intended," Dowcey said. "There are too many papers, we could not get her to the West Indies or Mexico. She would be missed and a search instituted."

Stockwell testified that Douglas ordered him to burn the papers. The crew divided up the captain's clothes and Dowcey pocketed Benson's gold watch. They agreed to head for shore and scuttle the ship. Spotting the beams of lighthouses in the darkness, they lowered the lifeboat and began to chop holes in the hull. After the head fell off the axe they were using, they abandoned the vessel and rowed to shore.

Douglas's lawyer, W.A. Johnston, cross-examined Stockwell when the trial entered its second day and tried to minimize his client's role in the mutiny. He established that both the mate and the cook had given orders and Douglas had seemed to be afraid of Dowcey "most of the time." Johnston challenged Stockwell's damning statement that Dowcey spoke to Douglas about taking the vessel to the West Indies "as we intended."

"I do not think that he [Dowcey] said 'as you intended,'" Stockwell replied, helpfully. Then he added, less helpfully: "He might have said so."

Dowcey was represented by Halifax lawyers W.A.D. Morse and John S.D. Thompson. It was the first major case for Thompson, a future Supreme Court judge who would become federal justice minister and, in 1892, succeed John Abbott as the country's prime minister. He had been practising for just three months and turned twenty during the trial. Given Stockwell's damning testimony, all the two lawyers could do was point fingers at Douglas. Questioned by Morse, Stockwell said Douglas and the captain "were not on the best of terms" and the mate had "growled" because he was forced to work on board while other crewmen went ashore during their last port visit.

Lambruert's lawyer, Robert Motton, established that Dowcey and Douglas had once sailed together on another vessel. But none of the defence lawyers had dented the main thrust of Stockwell's testimony – Dowcey had been covered in blood; he had apparently beaten the captain, possibly in collusion with Douglas; and Lambruert had helped to throw him into the sea while he was still alive.

Cross-examination "failed to shake him in the slightest degree," in the opinion of one newspaper reporter.

Stockwell's account was backed up by the remaining crewman, Marlbey. What's more, Marlbey testified, he had seen Dowcey speaking with Douglas on the day before the murder. Then, Dowcey had asked Marlbey to join their plot to throw the captain overboard and sell the ship and cargo. "At first, I thought it was only joking," he told the court through an interpreter. He had mentioned the discussion to Lambruert, who alerted the captain. Benson had thanked Lambruert for coming forward, but had not seemed to believe he was in danger. Less than twenty-four hours later, he was dead.

* * *

None of the defence lawyers called witnesses. In his summation, Morse argued there was "no positive proof" Dowcey had killed Benson. It was possible Douglas, as chief officer, was "the author and instigator of the bloody deed." Johnston, Douglas's lawyer, countered that his client was "doubtless a weak and cowardly man," but this did not make him a killer. He had gone along with the lie about the captain accidentally falling overboard out of fear of Dowcey, the lawyer asserted, and he had been the first to recant.

The chief justice gave his legal instructions to the jury on the trial's third day. Young stressed the evidence against Dowcey and he described the case against Douglas as "wholly circumstantial." If the jurors found that the two men had formed a plan to murder the captain, however, it would be a "mockery" not to hold him equally guilty of the crime. The jurors were back within two hours with their verdicts. Dowcey and Douglas were found guilty of murder. Lambruert, who had helped to dump the captain overboard, was acquitted.

Lawyers for the convicted men appealed. The Supreme Court dismissed Dowcey's bid to overturn the verdict on November 24, and he was sentenced to hang. As for Douglas, Johnston argued the evidence against him was so weak that the chief justice should have acquitted him, instead of allowing the jury to decide. The mate's sentencing was deferred until the appeal was decided.

On January 3, 1866, by a vote of four to one, the court upheld Douglas's conviction. The dissenting judge believed there was not enough evidence of his guilt, casting some doubt on the verdict. The next morning, the mate appeared for sentencing. Given a chance to speak, Douglas launched into a lengthy defence of his actions. "I am perfectly innocent of the crime, of which I have been falsely accused," one Halifax newspaper quoted him as saying. Douglas claimed he was asleep when Dowcey killed the captain. After Lambruert woke him up and told him what had happened, he entered Benson's cabin. Dowcey, "his eyes glaring," was standing over the body. "I was paralyzed at the sight and did not know what to do," Douglas told the court.

Douglas continued his story. He had left the cabin and had been approached by Marlbey, who asked him to take the vessel to the West Indies. "It flashed on me at once that there was a mutiny," he explained. "I trembled and thought to myself, 'my turn comes next.'" As for Stockwell, the prosecution's chief witnesses, "the young rascal was in the plot." Douglas said Dowcey asked him to help throw the captain's body overboard, but he refused. Dowcey then asked Lambruert, who turned to Douglas to ask permission. "Before I knew what I was about, I answered 'yes,'" Douglas said. "I knew I had done wrong in giving permission. I supposed he was dead all this time. If I had known there was a spark of life in the captain then, I would have died to have saved that spark."

Douglas said he convinced the crewmen the ship was too short-handed to reach the West Indies, and he steered a course for shore. He had hoped to reach a port and turn in the mutineers, but the crew decided to scuttle the ship. Douglas said he went along with the lie about the captain being knocked overboard by accident because Dowcey had threatened to kill him if he told the truth. "I had to yield to them. I took no command. Throughout, I knew my duty, wanted to do it, but had no power," he told the court, his voice choked with emotion. "I was more like a child than a man – no strength in me."

Chief Justice Young, noting that any respite would have to come from the government, sentenced Douglas to hang. Four days later, Dowcey summoned his lawyer, John Thompson, to his jail cell and dictated a lengthy statement. The belated confession was obviously calculated to prevent Douglas from escaping the gallows. "I am truly sorry for what I have done," Dowcey claimed, "but I did wrong because I was constantly persuaded to it by the mate."

Dowcey, in his statement, insisted that Douglas had been scheming against Benson all along, and had hatched the plot to kill him and take the vessel to the West Indies. Douglas had already recruited Stockwell and had asked Dowcey to try to convince one of the Germans to do the killing. While "I did not approve of it much," Dowcey said of the plan, he did as he was told. He was unable, however, to enlist a killer. Dowcey admitted he had struck and stunned Benson as he slept, then convinced Lambruert to help throw the body overboard.

Dowcey provided a horrifying description of what happened next. The water was calm and, as the crewmen discussed their next move, they could hear Benson splashing in the water and calling for help. When they emerged on deck he had cleared the stern and he was still struggling to stay afloat. Callously, they had stood and watched. "He deserved it. He was nothing but a rogue," Dowcey quoted Douglas as saying.

Despite Dowcey's last-minute allegations, the government commuted Douglas's sentence to life in prison at hard labour. One judge had expressed doubts about his guilt, and this appears to have been enough to justify sparing his life. "The hand that committed this cruel murder will soon be cold in death," Halifax's *British Colonist* noted when it reported the government's decision on January 19, "and society will be protected by the life-long imprisonment of his not less guilty accomplice."

Some four thousand people signed a petition asking for similar leniency for Dowcey. Hanging only Dowcey in the face of new evidence of Douglas's guilt would "create the impression of a partial failure of justice," defence lawyers Morse and Thompson argued. The government, although "strongly impressed with the guilt of Douglas," refused to spare the man who had, by his own admission, inflicted the blows and flung the helpless victim overboard. On January 24, 1866, a crowd of about two hundred gathered to watch Dowcey's execution. It was the last public hanging in Halifax.

Who was telling the truth, Dowcey or Douglas? Cowardice alone does not explain Douglas's actions. And since Dowcey lacked the skill to sail the ship, it seems unlikely he had acted on his own. Whatever Douglas's role in the murder of his captain, *Zero*'s mate would die in prison.

Part 4

Victorian Horrors

9

A Trust Betrayed

Wisps of smoke, slowly rising into the morning air from a pile of brush, first caught the attention of Isaiah Munro. He had spent the morning cutting hay with his brothers in an isolated meadow in the rugged country south of Annapolis Royal. Concerned the fire might spread, Munro wandered over to put it out. He later recalled that he "smelt meat burning" as he approached the smouldering brush, which covered a pile of stones.

Then he made the grisly discovery that would fascinate and repulse an entire province.

"Before I got there I saw a bone sticking through the rocks." Horrified, he ran back and told his brothers before heading into Annapolis Royal, about ten miles away, to summon the coroner. An autopsy would show the badly burned body was that of a woman in her thirties who was five months pregnant. Although she had been struck on the head with a rock, she was still alive when set on fire. The Halifax *Morning Herald* hardly exaggerated when, borrowing from *Hamlet*, it reported the crime in its September 2, 1880, edition under a headline that screamed "Murder Most Foul."

Suspicion immediately fell on a man seen driving a horse and wagon in the area only hours before the discovery. Locating that suspect became easy once the victim was identified as Charlotte Hill, an inmate of the poorhouse farm at North Range, a settlement some twenty-five miles to the west in neighbouring Digby County. Sheriff's deputies were dispatched to find the keeper of the poorhouse, a prosperous farmer named Joseph Nick Thibault – or Tebo, as the name was usually spelled by his anglophone neighbours.

"He was a very shrewd, intelligent man" despite a lack of formal education, having amassed several thousand dollars "by skilful cattle trading and similar speculations," the author of a history of Annapolis County noted. As one of many sidelines to farming, the forty-five-year-old Thibault was paid $300 a year by the North Range district, ten miles southwest of the fishing port of Digby, to look after paupers. Among them was Charlotte Hill.

Thibault was arrested on September 3 at the North Range farm, where he lived with his wife and children. A preliminary hearing was quickly convened at the courthouse in Annapolis Royal. Testifying before a courtroom described as "crowded to suffocation" with onlookers, poorhouse inmates confirmed that both Thibault and Hill had been missing from the farm on the night of August 31. Only Thibault had returned the following day. Other witnesses told of seeing Thibault travelling with a female companion at sunrise on September 1 and later spotting him alone.

Thibault pleaded not guilty to a charge of murder and was ordered to stand trial at the next sitting of the Supreme Court.

* * *

Thibault's trial more than a century ago ranks among the most sensational in Nova Scotia history. Hill's gruesome death and his position of trust as keeper of a poorhouse dictated that it would be no ordinary trial. The public was hungry for details. An enterprising photographer who took a tintype image of the dead

The courthouse in Annapolis Royal was the scene of Joseph Nick Thibault's 1880 trial for the murder of Charlotte Hill, a pauper who had been in his care. (Frederick Doig Photograph/Author collection)

woman's face sold about a hundred copies before the trial. Press coverage was extensive. *The Morning Herald* dispatched a reporter from Halifax to file, via telegraph, lengthy, verbatim accounts of the often lurid evidence.

The trial opened December 1 at Annapolis Royal, which had the distinction of being the site of the first court of English common law in Canada, circa 1721. Presiding over the latest chapter in the town's legal history was Justice Robert Weatherbe, forty-four, who was destined to become chief justice of Nova Scotia. At the time of his appointment, he was the youngest lawyer to be named to the Nova Scotia bench, and he had been a judge only two years when assigned the Thibault trial.

Underlining the seriousness of the case, Attorney General John S.D. Thompson chose to direct the prosecution in person. In those days the attorney general was expected to routinely handle cases in the Halifax courts. But prosecutions in the outlying counties usually fell to the most senior lawyer available – a tradition

Attorney General John Thompson, who would become Canada's fourth prime minister in 1892, led the prosecution team at Thibault's trial. (Library and Archives Canada C-068645)

that could be helpful to the defence, if no experienced lawyer could be found. The case against Thibault, based only on circumstantial evidence, was apparently judged too risky to leave in such uncertain hands.

Besides, Thompson probably relished the challenge. Only thirty-six, he had practised and taught law for fifteen years after his courtroom debut as defender of one of the mutinous crewmen of the ill-fated vessel *Zero*. He had been attorney general for two years, a stepping stone to the future posts of premier, Supreme Court judge, federal minister of justice, and, ultimately, prime minister of Canada. By 1880 he was considered the best legal mind in the province. "Given his mastery of his material, his lucid mind, he became nearly invincible in court," wrote biographer Peter Waite. Thompson's task was to marshal the strands of weak evidence needed to put a noose around Thibault's neck.

The prisoner was led into court and the trial began. Thibault "was closely shaven and coarsely dressed, wearing a striped sweater, which suggested penitentiary garb," reported *The Morning Herald*. "He has lost much flesh during his imprisonment and has a haggard look." He was defended by a trio of lawyers led by Robert Motton, an experienced criminal defender imported from Halifax. After an unsuccessful defence attempt to challenge the entire jury panel as biased, twelve men were chosen to try the case.

T.D. Ruggles, one of three lawyers assisting Thompson, opened the prosecution's case. He stressed the "horrible character" of the murder and set the scene for the jurors, suggesting that Hill had been burned alive "while the fiendish author of the crime stood by and gloated over her agony." The coroner, a Doctor Bungay, was the first witness and described the condition of the body. He rejected a defence contention that the blow to the head could have been caused by a fall. Other witnesses who knew Hill, including a half-brother, identified her from the remains and a photograph. They described a woman worn down by a life of poverty – short with stooped shoulders, a thin face, and several missing front teeth.

The final witness of the first day was Addie Scott, Hill's friend and fellow inmate at Thibault's poorhouse. She responded to the prosecutor's questions with silence until the judge threatened to jail her for contempt of court. Even then, she refused to positively identify the prisoner as Thibault. "She's been tampered with," one onlooker blurted out, prompting laughter among the spectators. Weatherbe moved swiftly to restore order, threatening to jail "at once" those responsible for further outbursts.

Scott proved no better as a witness when questioning resumed the following day. But Thompson "was marvellously patient
and gentle, and coaxed out of her, by degree, testimony about the
inmates of the [poor]house, Tebo's horses, carriages," one reporter wrote admiringly. She described how Hill had gathered up her
belongings in a borrowed basket before leaving the poorhouse the
night of August 31. On cross-examination Scott was more forth-
coming, telling the court that Hill had planned to run away. And
there was nothing suspicious about Thibault's absence that night.
He sometimes stayed overnight at another farm, she said. "It was
something for him to be home on a summer's night."

The prosecution called a succession of people who saw
a wagon carrying a man and woman early on the morning of
September 1. All described a man in dark hat and grey coat,
accompanied by a small woman, who passed by in a wagon
drawn by a dark horse. Within hours, they saw the man return
in the opposite direction, alone and "driving fast." Although they
identified the man as Thibault, his lawyer, Motton, forced a few to
admit that they could not be positive. But one man, Thomas Berry,
testified he had known Thibault for about nine years. They had
exchanged greetings as Thibault and the woman drove past.

The outdated system that had put Hill in Thibault's care
came under fire during the trial. Thompson's assistant, Ruggles,
criticized the "barbarous" practice, followed in some rural areas, of
putting paupers in the custody of the lowest bidder. An official of
the North Range poor district, John McNeil, testified that Thibault
had held the contract for just over a year. When the witness said
he did not know how many paupers had been in Thibault's care,
Justice Weatherbe became incensed.

"That is extraordinary," he snapped. "If they had been sheep
or cattle you would have had an accurate list."

By the trial's fourth day the prosecution had only a few loose
ends to tie up. Sheriff's deputies told of finding Thibault's horse
and wagon hidden in the woods. The Munro brothers described
finding the body. Thompson closed his case by calling Herbert
Rhoddy, who was hauling lumber not far from the scene of the

murder on October 18 when he spotted a partridge. Grabbing his gun, he chased the bird into a swamp and found a basket containing women's clothing and a photograph. The likeness was that of Charlotte Hill, the basket similar to one seen in Thibault's wagon the day of the crime.

The defence evidence was brief. Motton called three witnesses, two simply to establish that members of Thibault's family had been subpoenaed by the prosecution but did not testify. The third was a barber who shaved one of the prosecution's witnesses just before the trial. The man, he said, had bragged he was in town to "hang" Thibault. There was no effort to establish an alibi to counter the prosecution's strong circumstantial case.

The next day, December 5, Motton began his closing remarks. The attorney general, he asserted, was suggesting that "the prisoner had murdered the girl to cover up some shame and escape some expense," but "there was no evidence showing any improper relations" between Thibault and Hill. Motton charged that similarities in the evidence of many witnesses "showed that there had been some training somewhere" and he reminded the jurors of the "determined purpose in many minds to hang the prisoner." He finished by imploring them to acquit. "He was the bravest criminal ever known, if he were the man. Why had he travelled by daylight with the girl by his side? If he intended to murder her, would he have thus advertised the fact of his being in the girl's company?"

Thompson had an answer. "Men are never wise when they resort to crime," he said in the prosecution's summation. "Innocence is the only wisdom." As for the danger of convicting the wrong man, he argued that circumstantial evidence was persuasive. He used the example of a man seen entering a doctor's office and failing to emerge. The physician had been convicted of murder on the basis of a set of the man's false teeth, found among the ashes in a furnace. After reviewing testimony and the law for four hours, Thompson finished by contending it was not up to him to suggest a motive. But, he added, "there are many men with fewer temptations to commit crime than Tebo had, and many women as defenceless as Charlotte Hill."

Thompson's lengthy speech delayed the judge's charge to the jury until the following day. "The criminal selects his own time and place for the deed," Justice Weatherbe said, effectively excusing the prosecution's lack of direct evidence. The jurors, he added, should consider the fact that Thibault could have proved his whereabouts at the time of the offence, but failed to do so. If they had a reasonable doubt of his guilt, however, they should acquit.

* * *

The jurors began their deliberations at half-past one in the afternoon. "The stillness of death prevailed when at three o'clock the jury re-entered the courtroom," wrote *The Morning Herald's* reporter, not missing a chance to add to the drama. The verdict came as little surprise: guilty. All eyes swivelled to Thibault, who "sat like a statue," betraying no emotion until approached by his lawyer, Motton. "They have condemned an innocent man, sir," was Thibault's response to the verdict.

The court reconvened on December 7. Asked if he had anything to say before sentence was passed, Thibault again protested his innocence. The murder, Justice Weatherbe said, had been "attended by circumstances of brutality and cruelty ... God only knows what were your motives." Then he pronounced the sentence: death by hanging, to be carried out February 8, 1881. Thibault bowed his head and was led out of the courtroom.

Almost eight hundred people turned out for the execution, the first in Annapolis Royal in almost twenty years. Since executions were no longer carried out in public, the gallows in the jail yard was obscured by a twenty-foot-high wooden fence. An unruly mob, determined to see justice done, quickly tore it down. Guards reported that Thibault had paced the floor of his cell the previous night, but he appeared calm as he mounted the scaffold and the noose was fitted. The crowd fell silent as the trap gave way under his feet. Doctors declared him dead within minutes as spectators pressed forward for a better look.

Was Thibault guilty? Before the execution a story began circulating that Thibault had offered his version of events to friends. He had been taking Hill to another poorhouse on September 1 when they stopped to cook breakfast. Hill, who had threatened suicide in the past, suddenly threw herself into the fire. Unable to save her in time, Thibault had panicked and covered the body with brush and rocks, fearing people would assume he had killed her.

The story conveniently explained why Thibault had been with Hill before her death and why he had been seen fleeing the scene. But there was no evidence Hill had been distraught, let alone suicidal. And the idea that someone would kill themselves by leaping into a campfire seemed farfetched. Hill's pregnancy, if Thibault was the father, could have provided the motive that seemed so elusive during the trial. Would a man in Thibault's position resort to murder to try to avoid the expense and embarrassment of an illegitimate child? There seems no other explanation for the brutal killing of Charlotte Hill.

10

An Affair of Honour

Business was slow that Friday morning at Burchell's general store. With the Christmas season of 1853 barely over, the few people dropping in were more interested in the warmth of the woodstove than the goods on the shelves. Some regulars had already put in an appearance, complaining about the winter weather and filling the store with the sharp aroma of pipe smoke. But this was no ordinary day; Sydney was rife with scandalous rumours about a prominent young lawyer and the daughter of a respected citizen. George Burchell had heard the whispers, and he knew there was a tragic truth behind them. But he never suspected that the whole mess was about to come to a head in his shop.

When Nicholas Martin came through the door, Burchell was glad to see his old friend was in a good mood. He looked "calm and collected," Burchell thought – surprising, considering the strain he had been under. Sydney was a small town, and Martin, a former postmaster, a justice of the peace, and a gentleman farmer, was known to everyone. That was one of the reasons there was so much talk on the street. Martin and Burchell chatted about nothing in particular while another customer checked out the merchandise. But as soon as they were alone in the store, Martin revealed his real reason for stopping by.

Martin, a tall man of sixty whose brown hair was only now beginning to show a touch of grey, walked over to an open wooden keg filled with nails. He picked up one and asked the price. Four pence a pound, Burchell replied. Martin said he had recently bought two kegs and other hardware for renovations at his house about a mile from town. But he had "given up the notion," and now he needed money so he could leave Sydney with his daughter, Catherine.

Martin was about to ask Burchell if he would take the building materials off his hands when he was interrupted by the rattle of the front door. It was Alexander DesBrisay, a Wesleyan minister. The three men exchanged greetings and the conversation turned to the weather. A couple of minutes later Charles McAlpine, a merchant in town from Louisbourg and another mutual acquaintance, entered the store. Martin politely inquired about the health of McAlpine's brother, but he had more pressing matters on his mind. He took Burchell aside and asked if they could speak privately. Burchell accompanied Martin into the back part of the store, and closed the door.

Martin made his plea for cash. Burchell wanted to know how much he hoped to get for the nails and other building supplies, and balked when Martin said £70. Even if he wanted to buy them, Burchell explained, he did not have that kind of money on hand. Martin's face betrayed his disappointment.

"It's the only means I have of getting away," he said. "If I could sell the goods, I think I could get off on Captain Lewis's vessel," which was about to sail for the United States.

Burchell understood his friend's plight, but he had more bad news. He had just spoken with another mariner who said the Lewis ship did not have a cabin and was unlikely to take on passengers. Burchell suggested another merchant who might be interested in buying the goods, but Martin's options were growing fewer by the minute. He was trapped, unable to shield his daughter from the vicious gossip or take her away in a desperate bid to hide her pregnancy.

With that, Martin opened the door of the back room to leave. Burchell followed, but was shocked to see that someone had come into the store in their absence. There, standing at the stove with his back to them, was Archibald O. Dodd, Esq., a Sydney lawyer and, Martin was convinced, the source of all his troubles. Burchell feared a showdown, but Martin continued toward the door to the street, his hands in the pockets of his overcoat. He seemed oblivious to Dodd's presence.

Burchell walked a step behind and watched Martin's every move, alert for any sign that he intended to attack Dodd. "If I had seen Martin walk with a quick step, I would have seized him," Burchell claimed. But Martin continued toward the door at a normal pace. Dodd stepped away from the stove and, with his back still to Martin, headed toward the exit. It's possible he never saw Martin, who was a couple of steps behind him.

It was all over in seconds. Martin pulled a pistol from his right pocket, stepped forward, pressed the barrel against the back of Dodd's left shoulder and fired. An ear-splitting crack echoed through the store as Dodd doubled over and staggered toward the counter. Burchell saw a flash of sunlight reflect off the pistol as it was drawn, but he was unable to grab Martin in time. McAlpine and DesBrisay, who were still in the store, looked on in horror.

Burchell was the first to react. "How dare you do such a thing in my shop?" he screamed. "Go out. Go out." But Martin stood at the door with the smoking pistol in his hand, staring down at Dodd with what Burchell described as "a fiendish look" on his face. Burchell then grabbed Martin by the collar and pushed him backwards out the door.

"Now let the public take me," Martin declared as Burchell slammed the door in his face.

Burchell immediately turned his attention to Dodd, who was lying on his side behind the counter. He sent McAlpine and DesBrisay for a doctor, then eased Dodd onto his back and put a bundle of wrapping paper under his head as a makeshift pillow. Dodd was fading fast.

"It's no use," Burchell said as Dr. Lewis Johnston and McAlpine rushed into the store minutes later. "He is gone."

But as the doctor searched for a pulse, Dodd drew a breath. McAlpine took off again, this time to fetch Justice Edmund Murray Dodd and bring him to his son's side. The doctor opened Dodd's coat and discovered a pistol tucked inside. It was loaded, and Burchell gingerly placed the gun on a nearby shelf. Johnston unbuttoned Dodd's vest and shirt, revealing that the bullet had exited through the chest. But there was nothing he could do. Dodd was dead.

At almost the same moment, his killer walked into the nearby office of a justice of the peace, Peter Clarke.

"I have come to surrender myself to you," Martin, his face still flushed with excitement, announced as he took off his scarf. "I have had my revenge. I am a murderer. I have shot Dodd."

"Did you shoot him dead?" was the best response Clarke could muster to the startling admission.

"I saw him fall," Martin replied. He dropped to his knees in front of Clarke's desk and began to pray: "God have mercy on me for the act that I have done."

Just then Edward Archbold, a local merchant and one of Martin's closest friends, happened to walk in. Without a word of explanation, Clarke grabbed his coat, asked Archbold to keep an eye on Martin, and headed to Burchell's store to see for himself.

There were a few moments of uneasy silence, but Archbold sensed something terrible had happened. He was well aware of the bad blood between the Dodds and the Martins, and the reason Martin wanted so desperately to get out of town. Martin had been at Archbold's store earlier that morning, mean-mouthing the Dodds and trying to pawn off his building materials to raise money. Archbold had agreed to deliver a letter from Martin asking for passage on Captain Lewis's ship and that had seemed to do the trick. By the time Archbold had left Martin at the front door of Burchell's store, he had calmed down.

Now, less than an hour later in Clarke's office, Martin brought Archbold up to date.

"I have had my revenge," he explained.

"What do you mean?" Archbold asked.

"I have shot Dodd," he stated matter-of-factly, reaching into his pocket and pulling out the pistol to make sure Archbold believed him.

"My God!" Archbold exclaimed. "Which Dodd?"

"Archie."

"When? Where?"

"At Burchell's."

"Are you sure he is dead?"

"I fear he is," replied Martin. He asked Archbold to go to Burchell's to see if Dodd was still alive.

"You will know soon enough," Archbold said as he stood in the doorway to prevent Martin from leaving.

Martin displayed little concern about facing a murder charge, asking Archbold if he thought he could earn God's forgiveness by devoting the rest of his life to repentance and prayer. Within minutes, Deputy Sheriff Richard Logue – summoned once Clarke confirmed that Dodd was dead – arrived at the office. Martin stepped forward to offer himself for arrest.

"I know what you have come for. I am your prisoner."

Word of the execution-style shooting left Sydney's residents aghast. "This town was the scene yesterday morning of one of the most appalling Tragedies that it has ever fallen to our lot to record, and which deeply convulsed and agitated the whole community," Sydney's *Cape Breton News* declared in its New Year's Eve 1853 edition. The "shocking act," the paper tactfully reported, was apparently sparked by "an alleged injury done by [the] deceased to a member of the family of the accused." A coroner's jury had returned a verdict of willful murder the day of the killing, and Martin was in jail awaiting trial.

The newspaper's editor, James Ward, considered the slaying as a double tragedy. "We most sincerely grieve for and commiserate [with] the families of both parties," he wrote. Two of Sydney's most prominent and powerful families – the gentry, who were supposed to be setting an example for others – had resorted to violence to resolve their differences. But Martin's deadly act of revenge was shocking for another reason. In an age when a pregnancy out of wedlock was almost considered a crime in itself, the death of Archibald Dodd and the legal ordeal of Nicholas Martin exposed the repressive attitudes that pervaded Nova Scotia society in the Victorian era.

* * *

In the 1850s Sydney was a small port town with big aspirations. Its large harbour sheltered a steady stream of ships – square-riggers flying foreign flags and a fleet of locally built vessels – that carried timber and produce to international markets. The strategic importance of the harbour, located on Cape Breton's northern coast, had prompted the British to establish a garrison, further boosting the local economy. The town was laid out in a grid of streets at the tip on a peninsula jutting into a harbour, but it still had a rural feel, with fields between houses. "Sydney in the early days ... could justly lay claim to the possession of pretty homes and many beautiful gardens," one long-time resident claimed.

It would not be an exaggeration to describe Nicholas Henry Martin as one of the town's most popular citizens. Barely able to provide for his own family of eight, he was known for his generosity to others. "I never saw him turn his back on a poor man," declared a friend who, as a small boy, had been taken into the Martin household after his own father's death. An educated man given to quoting Shakespeare, Martin was also a staunch supporter of the temperance movement and sometimes lectured on the evils of drink. Unselfishness toward others, coupled with his normally quiet, sunny disposition, made people inclined to overlook Martin's less attractive features – bouts of depression and flashes of a temper.

Born in 1794 just outside Cork, on Ireland's south coast, he wound up in Cape Breton when his ship was wrecked offshore. He stayed and married. By the 1850s he was widowed and living with his six grown children on a farm near Sydney, known as Sun Lodge. Income from jobs as postmaster and justice of the peace made him comfortable, but far from wealthy. By 1853 he had handed over the postmaster's job to his eldest son, Robert, and turned his attention full-time to farming.

Martin doted on his children, and none more than Catherine, the younger of his two daughters. Even Kate's siblings agreed that she was his favourite. Martin described her to friends in glowing terms: "an amiable girl," he would say, "a more affectionate girl never breathed." One woman, a new acquaintance, claimed he spoke so often of Catherine that it was some time before she realized he even had another daughter. "I never saw so much devotion toward a child by a parent," she said. But there was a downside to this parental love – it made Martin strict and overprotective. Even though his children were getting older, he expected them to stay close to home. And like most young women of her time, Catherine was forbidden to be out at night without the "protection" of a chaperone.

The Dodds, unlike the Martins, did not need to earn respect; they commanded it with wealth and high office. Edmund Murray Dodd – war veteran, lawyer, politician, judge – was the scion of one of Cape Breton's most prominent families. His father had served as chief justice of Cape Breton when the island was still a separate colony. Born in 1797, Edmund Dodd joined the Royal Navy as a teenager. Just fifteen when war broke out with the Americans in 1812, he saw action as a midshipman and was locked up as a prisoner of war. He eventually followed in his father's footsteps, becoming a lawyer in 1821. He was elected to the Nova Scotia legislature in 1832, as the member for Sydney Township, and served as solicitor general before his appointment to the Supreme Court in 1848. "Despite his acknowledged ability as a lawyer, he was not a particularly successful judge," noted one biographer. "Increasing deafness combined with a tendency toward tedious and verbose explanation handicapped him."

Edmund Murray Dodd, a veteran of the War of 1812 and a Supreme Court judge, refused to believe that his son had assaulted the daughter of Sydney's former postmaster, Nicholas Martin. (Nova Scotia Archives Photo Collection)

When court schedules brought him back to Sydney – where he maintained a spacious estate in the centre of town, at an intersection nicknamed Judge's Corner – he conducted himself with the haughty bearing of a man accustomed to acting, and being treated, like a gentleman. A story was told of a time he went bird hunting with an officer from a French warship that was visiting Sydney. The Frenchman was about to shoot a snipe as it ran along the ground when Dodd stopped him. He was mortified at such a display of bad sportsmanship – shooting a helpless bird before it could take flight. "I'll never go shooting with a man of your stripe again," he said as he called his dog and headed home in disgust.

Not much is known about Archie Dodd. The judge's son had little time to make a name for himself before his fatal run-in with Martin. He had been practising law in Sydney for less than three years when he was gunned down at twenty-seven. But his family's wealth and prestige no doubt made him one of the town's most eligible bachelors. Witnesses at Martin's trial, few of whom were sympathetic to the Dodds, painted Archie as immature and a gadfly. And the evidence about to be revealed in a Sydney courtroom would sully his name forever.

* * *

It had been six months – six months of hell, six months of loneliness, six months of torture. And with every day that passed, Catherine Martin was finding it harder to hide the truth. How could she tell her father? It would be the death of him. And her brother, Robert, was likely to do something rash. She had to get in touch with Dodd. Maybe things could be put right. Maybe she could spare them all from the shame.

When Henry Forman, the family doctor, called at the Martin house three days before Christmas, Catherine realized it was time to share her secret. She managed to get a few minutes alone with Forman, and told him she was pregnant with Archibald Dodd's baby.

"She told me she had been very foolish herself, but did not charge [Dodd] with any violence," Forman would recall. Fearing they would be overheard, Catherine passed Forman a note bearing a set of instructions scrawled in ink. "I need to know what his intentions are," she whispered. Whether he liked it or not, Forman was being entrusted with the role of go-between.

"Tell that gentleman," the note said, "it would be better to marry, and for him to let me know on paper how he intends to act, but for God's sake say nothing about it to anyone else. Oh how foolish I have been." She asked Forman to meet her in private the following day to deliver Dodd's response.

If Catherine thought Forman would be her salvation, she was mistaken. The doctor was called away to attend to patients in the countryside over Christmas. Instead of delivering the note, he left it with her father's friend, Edward Archbold, for safekeeping. Forman later swore he did not reveal the note's contents to anyone; Archbold read it but agreed to keep it "a safe and profound secret."

But Catherine would not be able to keep her condition secret for much longer. She had been ill off and on since the late summer, and on Christmas Day she had "a violent fit," to use her sister's words. Dr. Forman was summoned, and used the opportunity to tell Catherine he had not conveyed her message to Dodd, and did not intend to. After the doctor left, Martin stayed at her bedside through the night. At some point, she finally told him the truth.

Martin was devastated. The next morning his other daughter, Mary, found him lying on his bed and "insensible." It took a dousing of cold water to wake him from his stupor. He said nothing to her or his other children about Catherine's condition, but Mary knew something was wrong. For the next five days Martin walked around in a daze, barely eating and sleeping. Friends were startled when he passed them on the street without saying a word, and his haggard appearance and erratic actions prompted some to remark that he must have lost his mind.

Martin became obsessed with saving Catherine's reputation. His first inclination was to take her far away so no one would find out she was pregnant. Without explanation, he packed her up on December 27 and headed into Sydney to take a steamer to New York. Mary went along to see them off. But the weather was poor, and the wind so strong that the steamer was unable to enter Sydney Harbour. The ship headed for its next stop without docking.

His plan foiled, Martin embarked on a new mission – ensuring that Dodd made amends for violating his daughter. The first step was to get the evidence down on paper. Justice of the peace that he was, Martin drafted a formal affidavit in which Catherine described how she had become pregnant. And she told her father exactly what he wanted to hear. She was not a fallen woman; Dodd, she now alleged, had raped her.

It had happened the previous June, she explained as her father used quill and ink to scribble down every sordid detail. She had been walking home on the main road from Sydney about dusk when she was overtaken by Dodd, who struck up a conversation. Suddenly, as they passed a path, Dodd seized her and dragged her into the woods. Then he threw her on the ground and as she tried to resist, he "raised up her clothes, and did violently and against her consent, perpetrate a rape on her body." Catherine said she had screamed for help until she fainted. When she came to, Dodd was still there. She had "cried bitterly" and threatened to tell her brother. Dodd, she said, had ordered her "to hold her tongue about it so no harm would follow."

Catherine became ill within days, and attributed the worst of her "fits" to the violence of the attack. Dodd had tried to rape her a second time on another occasion, she said, but she managed to fend him off. She swore she had not had intercourse with any other man before or since; the child's father had to be Dodd.

It was an extraordinary document – the sworn statement of a young woman forced to recount the details of her rape to her own father. But was it rape? Was it possible Catherine was too ashamed, or too scared of her father, to admit she had willingly had sex with Dodd? The pressure to paint Dodd as a fiend, and herself as a hapless victim, must have been intense. But Catherine stuck to her story. Later, when challenged in a courtroom about calling herself "foolish" in the note she gave to Dr. Forman, she insisted she had been "foolish" for "not telling my father when I was so ill treated."

* * *

Martin was more interested in protecting Catherine's honour than in seeing her attacker punished. The next morning, December 28, he headed into Sydney. Dodd was still in bed when Martin burst into the apartment behind his law office. Martin demanded that Dodd "make reparation for the wrong" he had done. Dodd's supporters later maintained that Martin was brandishing a large stick as he stood over Archie's bed; Martin denied being armed with anything other than the threat of a rape prosecution. Dodd, intimidated and rattled by the sudden intrusion, agreed to Martin's demand. "If Kate says that I am the father of the child," he said, "I will marry her."

Dodd asked for time to dress and promised to come to the Martin homestead to sort things out. Satisfied, Martin headed home. On the way he stopped to pick up his son Robert, who was surprised at how dejected his father looked.

"My God," Martin finally blurted out as their wagon lurched along the road, "Kate is ruined. She is in the family way by Archie Dodd."

Robert listened in disbelief as Martin described his encounter with Dodd. "The match would be a very bad bargain," in Robert's opinion. Martin agreed, but said he would do anything, even take on the job of Dodd's law clerk, and "soon make a man of him."

By the afternoon it was obvious Dodd had no intention of keeping the appointment, so Martin and his son went back into town. Dodd's office was empty; Martin took a chair in case Dodd returned while Robert tried to track him down. Finding Dodd in a town the size of Sydney proved easy, but getting him aside to discuss a matter of such delicacy was not. Robert waited impatiently in the cold as Dodd avoided him by chatting with a succession of lawyers and business associates. Finally, Robert spotted Dodd walking alone on the street and made his move.

"Why have you disappointed us?"

"I'm very busy this morning," was Dodd's lame reply.

"Do you intend to marry my sister?"

"I can't marry your sister," Dodd protested. "I'm engaged to another young lady."

Robert reported the exchange to his father, who was "thunderstruck." That evening, Martin decided to deal with the matter parent to parent. The judge was in his yard when Martin came to the fence and asked for a few moments of his time. Dodd, knowing why he had come, invited Martin inside to a room he used as his office. Dodd briefly fumbled through his desk for a match to light the candle, but the two men ended up sitting in the darkness.

"I want your son to make reparation for the wrong he has done my daughter," Martin began.

"I have no control over my son, he is not living in my house," snapped Dodd, who was no happier about the turn of events. "He has given me great dissatisfaction, but he denies the charge made against him."

"He can't deny it. I went to see him this morning, and he said he would meet me to arrange the affair." To Martin's mind, Dodd's initial promise to marry was an admission of guilt.

"My son was induced to make that promise under fear of violence," replied Dodd, as the discussion took on a hostile tone.

"I have not used violence. I don't intend to. I've warned Robert not to use violence," Martin replied. "I am going to act in a most cool and deliberate manner, and whatever the consequences the law must take its course."

"If my son is the guilty person you speak of," said Dodd, "I would not walk across the floor to save him from punishment. I recommend you put yourself in a lawyer's hands."

There was nothing left to discuss. Martin left the darkened office and walked home, his mind searching for some way to rescue his daughter from disgrace.

Martin spent part of the following day trying to raise money to take Catherine away from Sydney. While he seemed bent on leaving town, he continued to pressure Dodd into marriage. He asked a friend to deliver a note that could only be interpreted as a challenge to a duel. "Your vile conduct leaves me but one remedy," the note read. "Fail me not or I will brand you as a coward."

Edward Bown, who acted as Martin's messenger, was taken aback at Dodd's reaction to the note. "At first he treated it lightly," Bown recalled. "He told me he was guilty, but not to the extent charged by Mr. Martin." Dodd admitted having "improper intimacy" with Catherine, but claimed another man was the father of the baby. He asked for an hour to consult a friend – possibly his father – before drafting a reply. When Bown returned, Dodd handed him a scrap of blue writing paper bearing his terse response. "As I am not aware that my conduct toward you has been vile as you have stated," it read, "I would rather, before giving you the satisfaction you demand, have from you in writing the manner and way my conduct has been so."

It was a stalling tactic, and Martin was furious. "He was in a state of great excitement," Bown noted, when he delivered the note, and he felt Martin "had no control over his own actions."

That night Martin came into Robert's bedroom with more bad news – a neighbour had just told him that word of Catherine's pregnancy was all over town. This was hardly surprising, since for days Martin had told almost everyone he encountered that Dodd had violated his daughter. "We will be happy yet," Martin vowed.

The next morning, December 30, Martin was again at his son's door. He was heading into Sydney and wanted to borrow a set of pistols. Robert, who had heard gossip that Dodd was armed, handed them over so his father could protect himself. Within hours, Dodd was dead and Martin was facing the gallows.

* * *

The formal investigation into Dodd's murder began at the Sydney courthouse on New Year's Eve. Martin was still in sorry shape, and the lengthy hearing had to be delayed several times over the next few days because he was too ill to attend. At one point testimony was cut short when Martin had a seizure and collapsed on the floor. Several Sydney lawyers, displaying solidarity for a fallen comrade or fearful of offending a judge, declined to defend him. But by the time the hearing resumed on the third day of 1854, after hundreds attended Archibald Dodd's funeral, a rookie lawyer had agreed to take the case.

Dodd, however, had no trouble enlisting legal help as he set out to avenge a murder and protect his son's reputation. He sat through the entire proceeding with James McLeod, a Sydney lawyer and a member of the legislature. Since Dodd sat on Nova Scotia's highest court, the two magistrates conducting the inquest were not willing to challenge his right to seek the truth.

Dodd and McLeod peppered witnesses with questions and made sure nothing that painted Martin and his daughter in a bad light was overlooked. When the magistrates were finished examining Archbold, for instance, Dodd asked him to repeat what Martin had said when they spoke before the shooting. Martin had been raving about his treatment at the hands of the Dodds, Archbold admitted, and had described himself as "God's agent on earth to destroy that fellow." Archbold was not sure which Dodd he had been talking about. The judge had done some sleuthing and had convinced Dr. Forman to hand over the note in which Catherine chastised herself for being "foolish." It was entered as evidence.

The hearing was the first time Dodd and Martin had seen each other since their tense discussion in the judge's office. At one point, probably during a break as he was being returned to his cell, Martin confronted Dodd.

"If you, sir, had acted like a father, this dreadful occurrence would not have taken place," he declared. Dodd let the remark pass without comment. To Dodd's mind, shooting a man in the back was as cowardly as shooting a bird before it could take flight.

He would get his revenge by making sure Martin did not escape justice.

Even without the judge's intervention, there was enough evidence to send Martin to trial for murder. On January 4, after hearing from eight witnesses, the magistrates ordered Martin held in custody until the spring sitting of the Supreme Court.

* * *

Martin spent the next six months in the county jail, too sick to eat anything but oatmeal and eggs. He suffered more seizures. His daughter Mary came to his cell daily to look after him. Out of deference to Martin's place in the community he was locked up in a cell usually reserved for debtors, away from the convicted criminals. Once spring weather came, he was allowed to take short walks around the jail yard.

His trial was slated to begin in June 1854. But Solicitor General William Henry, who had arrived from Halifax to conduct the prosecution, was too sick to proceed. Defence lawyer Martin Wilkins, a prominent Pictou County politician who had taken the case in part because of his friendship with Martin, went on the offensive. Martin's health had deteriorated during his confinement, and defence witnesses had been assembled for the trial at great expense. And, Wilkins asserted, Martin had "a good and available legal and just defence" that could lead to an acquittal. The bottom line was that Martin should be released on bail to await trial. Martin filed an affidavit with the court declaring he was "unable to endure further imprisonment without manifest danger to his life." Martin's doctor and jailer agreed that confinement was taking its toll on Martin's fragile health.

The judge assigned to the case, Justice William DesBarres, had the final say. He agreed to the request to delay the trial, but balked at the idea of freeing Martin. The judge promised to return to Sydney within two months to conduct the trial at a special session of the court.

Defence lawyer Martin Wilkins argued that madness and "a fearful catalogue of provocations" had prompted Nicholas Martin to shoot and kill Sydney lawyer Archibald Dodd in 1853. (William Notman/McCord Museum I-44742.1)

The case of The Queen versus Nicholas H. Martin finally went to trial on August 10, 1854. It was an extraordinarily lengthy trial for the time – testimony and legal arguments stretched over eight days, with only one break to observe the Sabbath. Thirty-seven witnesses were called, almost half to testify in Martin's defence. The case drew enormous interest in Sydney and beyond. The courthouse, stuffy with the summer's heat, was packed each day. For those unable to get a seat, the weekly *Cape Breton News* suspended its normal diet of war news from the Crimea to provide a complete rundown of the evidence. Testimony filled column after column over a three-week period and continued to appear long after the verdict was known.

Justice DesBarres, a long grey beard hanging to his chest, could be forgiven for feeling awkward as he took his place on the bench. He had been appointed to the Supreme Court in 1848, a scant nine months after Dodd, and now he was presiding over the trial of the man who killed Dodd's son. DesBarres had close ties to Cape Breton – his grandfather had been the island's governor when it was a separate colony – but there's no evidence he was close to Dodd. Even if he were, he had a reputation for leaving his personal life at the courtroom door.

Years later, DesBarres would be remembered fondly as "kind-hearted and considerate ... a man of the highest honour and of incorruptible judicial integrity." More than anything, DesBarres was grateful to have made it back to Sydney alive. Shortly after adjourning Martin's case in June, he had narrowly escaped death when a small sailboat sank while ferrying him across the Bras d'Or Lakes. Justice DesBarres managed to cling to the wreckage until help arrived but another passenger, a Sydney lawyer accompanying him to court, drowned in the mishap.

Solicitor General Henry, recovered from his illness, presented the prosecution's case. Eyewitness accounts of how Martin shot Archie Dodd were repeated for the benefit of the jury. Wilkins showed his hand early – when it was his turn to question witnesses, he hammered away at how distraught and irrational Martin had been in the days leading up to the shooting. Wilkins mounted two lines of defence. He endeavoured to show that Martin was insane at the time of the slaying. Failing that, he hoped the "fearful catalogue of provocations" committed against Martin would encourage the jurors, as he put it, "to take the law into their own hands, as always happens in the case of homicide by dueling, and acquit him."

Wilkins expanded on the insanity defence when he opened his case on the trial's third day. At his prompting, Dr. Forman launched into a lengthy lecture on "homicidal monomania," a form of insanity in which a person affected is "irresistibly impelled to kill." In the doctor's opinion, Martin was "unsound in mind" when he killed Dodd.

It was August 15, the trial's fifth day, before Wilkins called the witness everyone had been waiting to hear. Nothing was said about Catherine Martin's baby in newspaper accounts of the trial, but the child must have been born the previous March. To help save her father from the gallows, she had to endure public confirmation of her unwed motherhood. Catherine was shown her affidavit charging Dodd with rape, which was read into the court record. Wilkins, who wanted only to establish the basis for Martin's attack, had no further questions.

But on cross-examination, Henry put Catherine's reputation on trial. Had she ever made "indecent overtures" to her father's friend, Charles McAlpine? Was it true that she once spent the night at a local house of ill-repute? Had she not been seen in the company of soldiers from the local garrison? Despite the onslaught, Catherine firmly denied each allegation.

But Henry had only begun his attack on her character. After the defence closed its case, he called more prosecution witnesses to rebut her testimony. They claimed Catherine had been keeping company with soldiers for several years, in particular a certain John Bird of the 42nd Regiment. Bird himself could not be called to testify because the entire Sydney garrison had been shipped out to bolster British forces in the Crimea.

On cross-examination, Wilkins chipped away at the credibility of each witness. Astonishingly, one man turned out to be an army deserter who was living at the Dodd home. Another witness, a woman, was a former Sydney bootlegger whom Wilkins accused of taking money in exchange for her testimony.

Undaunted, Henry forged ahead with his effort to impeach Catherine Martin. Dodd, who had outlined his dealings with Martin at the outset of the trial, was recalled for further testimony. Once, while walking in the woods, he claimed, he had spied Catherine "larking" with a soldier. "The one was chasing the other," he said, sounding as if he were still offended by the sight. "They were laughing immoderately." McAlpine, who witnessed Dodd's killing, testified that Catherine had once made "indecent overtures" to him, "in actions" rather than words. The message to the jurors was clear – no proper young lady would openly flirt with a man.

Henry closed his case a second time, only to find that the defence had a trump card to play. Wilkins had rebuttal evidence of his own, and called Sydney's jailer, Richard Logue, to muddy the waters. Logue testified that a local woman named Coolan "was so much like Kate Martin, in dress and appearance, that I myself once mistook the one for the other at a distance."

Wilkins and Henry needed a full day to sum up their cases, and it took Justice DesBarres another day to review the evidence and the law. Finally, at five o'clock on August 18, the jurors filed out to begin their deliberations. Two hours later, with no break for dinner, they returned with a verdict. Sydney residents who were lucky enough to get seats in the courtroom left no doubt whose side they were on once the verdict was announced. The foreman had barely said the words "not guilty" when he was drowned out by cheers and applause.

Once Justice DesBarres restored order, the solicitor general proposed that the jurors be asked the ground for the acquittal – an unusual move to close out an unusual trial. Wilkins protested that the verdict had been properly recorded and the case was no longer in the jury's hands. The judge, however, seemed to want to satisfy his curiosity. Wilkins later claimed only "some" of the jurors said they found Martin not guilty by reason of insanity.

Justice DesBarres, however, recorded this as the unanimous verdict. Wilkins sputtered that the court "had no right to order a sane man to be detained in custody on the ground of insanity," but the judge was unmoved. He ordered Martin to remain in jail until the government decided his fate. The final verdict would be decided in the corridors of power in Halifax.

* * *

The applause that greeted the verdict showed public opinion was on Martin's side in his hometown. And he was attracting supporters among opposition politicians looking for fresh ammunition to attack the government that had prosecuted him. On September 4, two weeks after the trial, a Halifax newspaper allied with the opposition was confident that "the warrant for Mr. Martin's release only awaits the signature of the governor."

But the government was unsure how to proceed. While there was a law dealing with the criminally insane in Britain, none existed in Nova Scotia. The government was thought to have the power to detain, for an indefinite period, someone found criminally insane. The chief justice, Brenton Halliburton, took this view when the government sought his advice. And there was another factor to consider – Dodd informed the governor that he feared for his life if his son's killer were set free. As William Young, the premier and attorney general, put it, the government was caught in "a most delicate and painful position." Faced with evidence suggesting Martin was dangerous as well as insane, Young elected to leave him behind bars.

Stymied at the political level, Martin's lawyers filed a writ of habeas corpus to have the courts declare his detention illegal. The motion, demanding Martin's immediate release, came before the Supreme Court's full bench – the appeal court of the time – in Halifax in late November. While Dodd was barred from taking part, there was nothing to keep Justice DesBarres from hearing the motion, even though his conduct was under fire. Surprisingly, judges were free to take part in appeals arising from their own trials and could vote on the outcome.

Wilkins filed an affidavit from Dr. Forman, who claimed that since the trial Martin had "continued to be perfectly sane and in his right mind, without any symptom of mental alienation." In his opinion, Martin no longer needed to be locked up to protect the public. But the most startling documents put before the court were affidavits from four of the twelve jurors, including foreman Paul Murphy, contending that their verdict had been an "unconditional" not guilty. What's more, three of these four denied that Justice DesBarres asked them the reason for the acquittal in the confusion that followed the announcement of the verdict.

Martin's defenders were trying to have it two ways. The Supreme Court was being asked to free Martin because he had been acquitted of murder. If the court felt not guilty by reason of insanity was the proper verdict, then Martin should be released because he was now sane. These were the arguments Samuel Fairbanks, a prominent lawyer and one of Wilkins's political allies, brought before the court on November 26, 1854. The reception was hostile. The chief justice, Halliburton, immediately turned the floor over to Justice DesBarres, who rejected the jurors' claims. The foreman, Murphy, had clearly said the acquittal was based on insanity, Justice DesBarres maintained, "and most of the other jurors gave the same answer, none of them expressing their dissent."

Then each judge in turn offered his views on the case. The chief justice acknowledged that there was no statute on the books in Nova Scotia dealing with the criminally insane, but argued the common law empowered the government to detain people acquitted by reason of insanity. "It would be monstrous if the government had no power to keep a prisoner in custody in such circumstances," Justice William Blowers Bliss added. "If not, a raving maniac might be let loose on the community." Justice Thomas Chandler Haliburton, who was on the verge of fleeing the bench to pursue his second career as an author and satirist, warned that the courts could face more insanity defences in the future if Martin were released. "I think the discharge of the prisoner on the ground of his sanity, when the jury have found him to be insane, would be a precedent dangerous to the peace and security of the community." Justice DesBarres made it unanimous. Martin's incarceration was lawful, he said, and any further effort to have him freed should be directed to the government.

* * *

When the legislature's spring session opened a little over a month later, Wilkins tabled a petition from Martin and a stack of other documents relating to the case. On February 7, 1855, he rose in the House of Assembly and launched into a speech outlining his client's legal ordeal. For Martin, who had been behind bars more than a year, it was his last hope for freedom. But for Wilkins, a member of the Tory opposition, it was also a chance to take potshots at the Liberal government. A skilled debater, he was as at home in the assembly as in the courtroom. While colleagues grudgingly acknowledged his skill as a lawyer, many found Wilkins's bombast hard to stomach. He was grossly overweight, leading one wag to dub him Falstaff, after the comic Shakespearean character of similar girth.

Wilkins attacked Justice DesBarres for refusing to set Martin free, and took a swipe at Dodd for spearheading the drive to keep his client off the streets. But he saved much of his venom for the solicitor general, Henry, whom he accused of conducting a "persecution" rather than a prosecution. Witnesses drawn from the ranks of "the lowest of the low ... perjurers and deserters" had been hauled into the courtroom to sully the reputation of Martin's daughter.

Henry welcomed the chance to refute rumours that had been circulating for months. Wilkins, he charged, had bullied the prosecutors and Justice DesBarres throughout the trial, just as he was now trying to bully the government. As for the treatment of Catherine Martin, Henry said he had warned Wilkins that he had witnesses to contradict her evidence if she testified. "If unpleasant disclosures were made," Henry contended, "the learned member himself caused them."

Martin's cause received some high-profile support from the government benches, underlining the divisions caused by the case. "I pity the one father as much as I do the other," said the formidable Joseph Howe, a cabinet minister. "Both will wear these scars to the end of their days." While Howe had little time for Wilkins – he once dismissed him as a coward and a braggart – he expressed sympathy for Martin's plight. He challenged his fellow politicians to put themselves in Martin's shoes, and ask what they would have done in his situation. "Had I been on that jury," Howe contended, "I would have pronounced him not guilty, as I believe these twelve men did. If they were fathers, and had daughters of their own, if they were men at all, they could not have given, under the circumstances, any other verdict." The government had a duty, he said, to order Martin's release.

That brought the premier and attorney general, William Young, to his feet. Faced with an insanity verdict, at least on the official record, the government had a duty to keep Martin in jail, he told the legislature. However, "if anything can be done to relieve this gentleman from incarceration with propriety and safety," Young added, "I shall be glad." The debate dragged into the evening, but finally a consensus was reached – a new jury would be empanelled to decide, once and for all, if Martin should be detained as a lunatic or freed as a sane man.

* * *

A government-appointed commission to rule on Martin's sanity opened its hearing in Halifax on March 13, 1855. A group of opposition politicians escorted him into the packed courtroom. After a round of handshakes with supporters in the gallery, Martin was afforded the courtesy of sitting with his lawyers rather than standing in the prisoner's dock. Despite his constant complaints of ill health, he seemed to have held up well in jail. One newspaper reporter was struck by "his erect and manly bearing," which suggested "a man of high education and sensitive feelings."

After a twelve-member jury was chosen, Attorney General Young pointed out that the hearing would be the first of its kind in the province. And with new laws about to be introduced in the legislature to deal with the criminally insane, it would be the last. "If Mr. Martin is acquitted now and set at liberty, it will be fortunate for him that the provisions of the English statutes" – authorizing detention of those acquitted on the grounds of insanity – "were not in operation before." There was no doubt Martin had killed Archibald Dodd; the only question for this new jury was whether he was now sane.

Wilkins, stubborn to a fault, opened his case with an attack on Young for assuming Martin was insane in the first place. He produced six doctors who had examined his client and swore he was sane. But none of the physicians displayed any special knowledge of insanity, and their opinions were based more on conventional wisdom than science. "A child will detect an insane person," one claimed. "I could tell from his appearance, his eye, and the expression of his countenance [that] Mr. Martin is now perfectly sane." Young did not dispute their findings. His goal was to establish that none of the medical men thought that Martin would be a danger to others if released.

The jurors declined an offer to question Martin themselves. After a few minutes of whispered deliberation in the jury box, the foreman declared that they had found Martin "not insane." There was a burst of applause in the gallery, and a throng of supporters gathered around Martin as he emerged from the courtroom, a free man for the first time in more than fourteen months. "We sincerely congratulate Mr. Martin's friends in Sydney on the termination of his long and cruel punishment," the editor of the *British North American*, a Halifax newspaper, wrote approvingly, "and trust that he will soon be restored in good health to the bosom of his family."

The law was finished with Martin, but the wounds opened by the killing of Archie Dodd were not easily healed. Five months after his release, Martin attended a clergyman's lecture in Sydney. Dodd was already in the audience and, shortly after Martin took his seat, he rose – along with a number of his friends – and walked out. Martin fired off a letter to the minister apologizing for the disruption, and seized the chance to defend his conduct.

"To my God I appeal that the crime I was charged with never for a moment entered my thoughts," Martin wrote. "Reason left her abode, and I knew nothing of my miserable situation until I found myself inside the walls of a prison." But even if he had killed in a fit of temporary insanity, as he seemed to be suggesting, Martin had no doubt that he had done the right thing. "I feel confident my prayers have been heard. My life has been spared, my health is good, and I sleep quiet and sound without the shadow of the fatal deed ever crossing my thoughts."

The popular support for Martin and the release of his son's killer would have been galling for Dodd. He must have felt that the justice system he was sworn to uphold had failed his family. He remained on the bench another twenty years; a lacklustre judge at the best of times, he was openly ridiculed in the press as old age began to take its toll. He finally retired in 1873, three years before his death at seventy-nine.

Nicholas Martin lived out his days at Sun Lodge, "respected and beloved by all who knew him," according to one observer. He was eighty-seven when he died in January 1881, almost three decades after honour or madness – and perhaps both – drove him to murder.

11

Death at the Polls

TO THE POLLS, MEN! TO THE POLLS!
Go at it today, in right good earnest. Go at it in right good humour.
Spare no effort to win. Do to those opposed to you as you would be
done by. Maintain your rights. But do so peaceably. Give no offence.
Take no offence. Take, but give no insults. Poll your votes. Poll them
every one. Give no cause of provocation. Act like men who know
what their rights are, and know how to maintain them. Be sober,
be vigilant.
                          – The Morning Chronicle, Halifax, May 12, 1859

Passions were running high as hundreds of men descended on the tiny community of Grand Lake on May 12, 1859, to cast their ballots. This was no ordinary Nova Scotia election – it was a fight for political supremacy between Catholics and Protestants. And in the midst of fields and farms clustered on the shore of Grand Lake, some fifteen miles north of Halifax, the struggle was about to erupt into open warfare.

All morning, men – only men had the right to vote – had been filing in and out of the polling station. Across the road at

White's Hotel, the upstairs had been rented by the opposing parties to refresh their troops. Liberals quaffed ale, ate, and talked politics in one room; next door, the hated Tories did the same. Many were spoiling for a fight. Patrick Hurley and Bryan Kennedy, two burly Irish railway workers, led a group of Tories who shoved their way into the Liberals' room. One man was struck in the face with a tumbler and cut before James White, the hotelkeeper, stepped in and ordered the Tories out.

Outside, whenever Tories and Liberals crossed paths, threats or insults were exchanged. Scuffles broke out. At one point, Liberal supporters George Preeper and George Gray were leaning out a second-storey window of the hotel as Hurley and another man, John Carroll, walked below.

"Draw in your head, you Protestant son of a bitch," Hurley shouted.

"You damn Catholic son of a bitch," Gray shot back, shaking his fist. That did it. When Gray came out of the hotel a few minutes later, he was jumped and beaten by a gang of Tories. When another Liberal, Thomas Lowrie, tried to intervene, the attackers turned on him.

About a dozen Liberals, including Preeper, decided enough was enough. They ran up the road to the farm of James Kenty, where rifles and shotguns had been stashed earlier in the day. Heading back to White's Hotel to save their comrades, they were met by upwards of a hundred Tories, some wielding sticks and rocks.

"The two parties were in an attitude of war," noted one man who ran for cover.

"Stay back," shouted one of the armed men. Another fired a shot into the air but the Tories, emboldened by liquor and their superior numbers, kept advancing. They overran the Liberals, grabbing guns and breaking them. Some Liberals were beaten with the stocks of their own rifles; the rest retreated a few yards and turned to make a second stand. Hurley lunged for Preeper's gun. Preeper scrambled onto a pile of logs and raised a double-barrelled shotgun to his shoulder. Hurley was still coming at him as Preeper fired. He collapsed, blood pouring from a gaping wound to his neck, and bled to death within minutes.

Preeper fled into the woods. The Tories, seeing one of their number dead, savagely beat the handful of Liberals who were unable to escape, including the party's scrutineer, who had remained at the polling booth and took no part in the riot. Miraculously, Hurley was the only fatality of one of the darkest days in Nova Scotia electoral history.

* * *

Violence often marred elections in nineteenth-century Canada. Partisan combat was a form of warfare, with thugs recruited to intimidate or attack supporters of rival candidates. And the results could be deadly. During Nova Scotia's 1830 election, a gang armed with sticks started a riot, leaving one man dead. But the province had yet to witness an election that equalled the bitterness and hatred of the 1859 campaign.

At stake was something graver than the usual disagreements over railway-building or public expenditures; the rallying cry was religion. "This election," noted Nova Scotia's top political historian, J. Murray Beck, "was the only one in provincial history primarily fought and decided on the religious question." It was an all-out battle for political power, waged between Protestants and Catholics.

Sectarian tension had spilled over into the political arena in the mid-1850s. Acadian and Scottish Catholics were uneasy within the ranks of the Liberal government after Premier William Young, bowing to Protestant pressure, withdrew a proposal for separate Catholic schools. When the House of Assembly opened in February 1857, they made their move. Eight Catholic members crossed the floor and Young's government fell on a non-confidence motion. James W. Johnston, the Conservative leader, formed a new administration that was dependent on Catholic support. The newspapers of the time openly supported political parties, and the

Liberal press condemned Johnston as a sell-out who was under the thumb of a Catholic minority bent on imposing its will on the Protestant majority.

By the time Johnston went to the polls in the spring of 1859, emotions were at a fever pitch. Each side blamed the other for starting the strife. The highly partisan press of the day pleaded for order on election day, but in the same breath spread fear and suspicion. *The British Colonist*, the government paper, reported that an opposition politician had advised Liberal supporters to arm themselves. *The Novascotian*, the Liberals' Halifax newspaper, called the charge "a base, black slander," but warned its readers that "a row, on Election day, is almost certain to lead to a riot. A riot in this City, just now, might end in a conflagration or other terrible disaster – perhaps the loss of life or some fearful calamity."

It took several days to tally the votes and declare the winners. Telegraph lines between Halifax and several outlying counties were down, leaving the outcome in doubt. Two days after the polls closed *The British Colonist* predicted "a decided majority" for the government. It was wishful thinking. The Liberals, riding the Protestant backlash against the government, won a narrow majority, twenty-nine of fifty-five seats. "The Government is beaten. Soundly beaten," *The Novascotian* proclaimed on May 16. "Nova Scotia is herself again … She has thrown off the yoke of tyranny … Nova Scotia, Protestant Nova Scotia, is free."

Among the victorious Liberals were John Esson, a merchant, and publisher William Annand, whose newspaper holdings included *The Novascotian* and *The Morning Chronicle*. The pair defeated the government candidates, Falconer and Gladwin, by some seven hundred votes in the eastern division of Halifax County. But their election was overshadowed by Hurley's death and the rioting within their constituency, at Grand Lake. In voting that was cut short by the riot, the Tory candidates took seventy-eight and seventy-nine votes at the village's poll, compared to thirty-five and thirty-four respectively for Esson and Annand.

The *Colonist* condemned Hurley's shooting as "cold-blood-ed, premeditated and cruel murder, perpetrated with the view of driving from the polls the friends of Messrs. Falconer and Glad-win." *The Novascotian*, predictably, accused the government of sparking the violence by importing Irish-Catholic railway workers to vote for its candidates. The *Acadian Recorder*, pro-Conservative despite its claims of independence, called the incident "the darkest page in the history of such contests that Nova Scotia can produce since this Province has had a House of Assembly."

* * *

More shrill rhetoric was to come in the weeks following the election. The Conservatives charged that the opposition had used bribery, intimidation, lies, vote-buying, and "every species of row-dyism" to win. The Liberals fired back, claiming the government had bought votes with gifts of boots, hats, shawls, and rum – and some of its supporters had voted more than once. According to *The Novascotian*, one Irishman, asked if he was planning to vote, had replied: "Och, by jappers, and isn't it tired of voting I am?" And the Catholic clergy, it was said, had instructed members of their congregations to vote Conservative or face excommunication.

As the war of words raged in the press, George Preeper and nine others were charged with murder. Preeper and brothers John and James Kenty turned themselves in shortly after the shooting and were jailed; the other seven remained at large.

The next sitting of the Supreme Court in Halifax was set for the fall of 1859. In July, Preeper petitioned the lieutenant governor, Lord Mulgrave, seeking a special session of the court to hear his case sooner. His health had been "greatly impaired" by two months behind bars, Preeper claimed, and he was "one of a large family who are unfortunate in having a dissipated Father, and ... had been of late years the chief support of his Mother and [her] six small children." Adding that he was "entirely innocent" of the charge, he asked for an early court date to establish his innocence. The Kenty brothers filed a similar request.

The petitions were forwarded to the courts, but Chief Justice Brenton Halliburton had been reading the newspapers. "It would be injudicious to hasten the trial," he replied on July 22, "as it is more probable that Justice would be done both to the public and the prisoners if it took place at the usual sittings of the Court in October next, where a longer time would have elapsed for the public mind to cool, after the excitement apt to exist on both sides upon so sad an event." The three men languished in prison for three more months.

The timing of the trial was crucial, as it determined how strongly the prosecution would press for a conviction. Despite the government's defeat at the polls, the Conservatives were in no hurry to hand over the reins to the Liberals. The party would cling to power until the legislature met in January 1860, and only then would it be voted out of office by the assembly's Liberal majority. In the meantime it was business as usual; James W. Johnston, who was attorney general as well as premier, handled the prosecution. Since the victim, Hurley, had been a Conservative supporter, the Crown went all-out in its effort to send the accused to the gallows. Had Preeper's party taken office immediately after the election, the case would undoubtedly have taken a different course.

The first step was to have the charges reviewed by a twenty-four-member grand jury, which would hear testimony and determine if there was enough evidence to send the accused to trial for murder. If the grand jurors were not convinced there was sufficient evidence of a crime, they could refuse to issue indictments and the prosecution would cease. Justice William Blowers Bliss, probably the keenest legal mind on the Supreme Court, instructed the grand jury on October 27, reminding them that "if a number of persons were assembled together, and one committed murder, the others aiding and abetting, all were equally guilty of the crime." The grand jury – only seventeen strong, because of no-shows – returned true bills against all ten accused.

Justice William Blowers Bliss believed it would be "a solemn mockery" of justice to put as many as ten election day rioters on trial for murder. (Author collection)

Liberal Party leader William Young was poised to reclaim the premier's office when he defended a man who killed a political opponent during a riot at the polls in 1859. (Notman Studios/Nova Scotia Archives No. 1983-310/50480)

But the prosecution ground to a halt when the three men were arraigned the following week. Defence lawyers William Young, who was poised to reclaim the premier's office, and Jonathan McCully, another prominent Liberal, announced they had proof only nine of the seventeen grand jurors had agreed to return the true bills. The law required the agreement of at least a dozen grand jurors for charges to proceed.

Another Supreme Court judge, Justice Lewis Morris Wilkins, had to sort out the mess. Grand jury proceedings were supposed to be secret, and some lawyers questioned whether the vote could be revealed in court. Justice Wilkins agreed, ruled he could not investigate a questionable grand jury vote, and forged ahead with the trial. Preeper and the Kenty brothers, still the only three in custody, pleaded "not guilty under protest," and the trial was set to begin the following week.

But Justice Wilkins, who was only in his second year on the bench, took advantage of a recess to run his decision past the chief justice, Brenton Halliburton, and Justice Bliss. No lack of judicial expertise there – the octogenarian Halliburton had been on the bench for more than five decades, Justice Bliss for twenty-five years. Wilkins, advised to deal with the defence concerns, returned to the courtroom and announced that "substantial justice might be defeated altogether ... especially in a case of life and death" unless the grand jury was resummoned. Grand jurors, he ruled, could disclose an error in their verdict without revealing the substance of their deliberations.

Eight days later, the court reconvened. The grand jurors had been rounded up and foreman William Metzler admitted it had voted nine to eight to hand down the murder indictments. Justice Bliss, who accompanied Justice Wilkins to court for the hearing, said it would be "a solemn mockery" of justice to proceed with a trial. The murder indictment against Preeper, the Kentys, and the seven men still at large was quashed.

Attorney General Johnston promptly submitted a new one charging the same ten men with the less serious offence of manslaughter – an unintentional homicide. The jurors reheard the evidence and returned an indictment against only Preeper. The Kenty brothers were freed and Preeper's trial was set to begin November 14. If convicted, he faced a fine or a prison term of up to fourteen years.

* * *

"The case is one necessarily of a political character," defence lawyer McCully, a thin-faced man with long sideburns that dangled from either side of his head, contended as Preeper's trial began. "The whole difficulty arose between two political parties." The case was, indeed, all about politics. The venue, the Supreme Court's hearing room in Province House, was just one door down from the legislative assembly's chamber. Tory lawyers sat at the prosecution table, rival Liberal barristers appeared for the defence. And partisanship coloured the testimony of almost every witness.

Two stories emerged about what had happened on election day at the Grand Lake polling station, split along political lines. The prosecution's dozen witnesses, all but one of whom had voted Tory, painted a picture of harmless railway workers suddenly challenged by a group of unruly Liberals armed with guns. They had attacked the Liberals, they claimed, only to disarm them. The twenty or so witnesses called by the defence – most had voted Liberal – told a different story. The railway workers, they said, had been spoiling for a fight all day, intimidating Liberal voters with insults and threats. When the Liberals fetched their guns to protect themselves, the riot erupted and George Preeper killed Patrick Hurley in self-defence.

The defence version seems closer to the truth. Consider the evidence of Bryan Kennedy, a prosecution witness and employee of the government-owned railway. Questioned by the attorney general, Kennedy said the Tory supporters marched toward the Liberals and told them to put down their guns. When they refused, the Tories began taking the guns away. Kennedy said he carried a stick but claimed he was the only Tory carrying a weapon of any kind. He said nothing about having used it.

Cross-examined by McCully, Kennedy admitted he had heard there might be trouble, so he had stashed the stick under White's Hotel earlier in the day. Yes, he conceded, he had used the stick during the riot, knocking down several Liberals. And yes, he had gone for Preeper but had slipped and fallen before reaching him. Even so, he had managed to give Preeper a glancing blow to the head. This was moments before Hurley was shot. And in the wake of the shooting, Kennedy conceded, the Tories took revenge on a handful of Liberals who were too badly injured to run away, beating them even more. "Some of our side wanted to kill them," Kennedy told the defence lawyer, "and others wouldn't let them." For his part, Kennedy seized one of the injured men and dragged him by the hair.

Once the defence began presenting evidence, the focus shifted to events leading up to the shooting. Philip Brown, an agent for a canal company, said when he visited White's Hotel to pick up some of his employees, two Tory supporters struck him from behind. "These men were going about evidently striving to kick up a row." One of the men asked Brown if he was going to vote. Brown said he wasn't. "In God's name you had better not," the man warned, "for if you do, you had better prepare your coffin." In contrast, Brown testified, the Liberals "behaved in a great orderly manner."

In the wake of the shooting, the Liberal press had charged that the government had sent its railway workers to Grand Lake to disrupt the voting. Defence evidence seemed to substantiate the allegation. James Hunt, a conductor on the Nova Scotia Railway, testified his train picked up at least twenty-five railway workers at various stations between Halifax and Grand Lake on the morning of the election. More arrived by train from the opposite direction. All were carried free, Hunt said, by order of a high-ranking railway official.

More damning was evidence that the government had paid the railway workers for election day, even though they were given the day off to vote. Other defence witnesses refuted the claim that the workers were unarmed. Several witnesses said the Tories carried rocks, sticks, and crowbars; some maintained Hurley, the man who died, had rocks in his hands as he lunged at Preeper.

To establish that the Liberals had reason to fear that violence could break out, the defence called John Kenty. He described how three railway workers had come to his house a week before voting day and had threatened to beat him because he was canvassing for the Liberals. Kenty had been struck across the head before he could escape. On election day, a group of Liberals had showed up and asked Kenty, who lived just up the road from White's Hotel, to store their guns in case there was trouble. Kenty had let them put the guns, hidden in rolled-up rugs and quilts, in a spare room. Kenty had served as a Liberal scrutineer at the polls, until railway workers threatened him again. "I was frightened for my life," he said, and had fled, with his wife and children in tow, moments before the shooting started.

The biggest obstacle for the defence was the man surveying the courtroom from the bench. Justice Wilkins, a tough and opinionated judge, had been appointed by the Liberals in 1856, but he came down hard on McCully and Young, who were former cabinet colleagues. He was either trying to prevent any appearance of favouritism or had abandoned his partisanship when he assumed judicial office. Then again, the judge might have been having trouble deciding which party he favoured. He had started his political career as a Conservative, jumped to the Liberals, then returned to the Tory fold, only to switch to the Liberals in return for the judgeship he had long coveted.

During Kenty's testimony, Justice Wilkins interrupted when he felt the witness was straying too far from the events of election day. He did not mince words. "I must say that the defence in this case had been conducted in a manner most discreditable to a British Court of Justice," he snapped. McCully and Young protested that they had to show that the Liberals had grounds to bring guns to protect themselves. After a brief, heated argument, the judge relented.

Justice Wilkins devoted most of his instructions to the twelve-man jury to a scathing attack on McCully's assertion that the trial was a political one. "I will not insult you by the supposition that you could possibly be induced to regard this case as a political question, or to permit any other influences to affect your deliberations than grave and matured considerations of duty," he told the jurors. "If you and I could be brought to prostitute our offices in the Temple of Justice to political partisanship ... what security would a Colonial subject have for his property, his liberty, his life?"

The Liberals, the judge contended, were not justified in taking up arms to defend themselves. But for the evidence that Hurley was holding rocks when he went after Preeper, the judge said bluntly, the defendant would have been guilty of murder. And there was no question of his guilt on the manslaughter indictment. "I am bound to say, the law and the evidence, in any view of the facts in proof," Justice Wilkins emphasized, "constrain you to find him guilty."

Whether the jury would heed the judge's direction to convict was another question. The Tory press later charged that the bulk of the jurors were Liberal supporters; the foreman, Charles Tropolet, was described as "perhaps the most inveterate radical" – read die-hard Liberal – in Halifax.

The jurors' sympathy for Preeper became obvious as the judge began reviewing the testimony. "Gentlemen," Justice Wilkins said, looking up from his notes, "I perceive from the listlessness and indifference which some of you are exhibiting that I am performing ... a useless labour. I am reading over these long notes, not for my amusement, but for your information. Be so good," he added, his voice dripping with sarcasm, "as to tell me whether you wish me to proceed?"

There was a long pause. "I believe the jury feel that they already know enough of the case," replied Tropolet, proving himself one of the bravest foremen ever to lead a jury.

Wilkins snapped shut his notebook. "I have the honour to sit here as a British Judge," he began, barely containing his anger. "I have a deep sense of the obligations which attach to that office. I have endeavoured, in this exciting and important cause, to discharge them truly and correctly ... My duties and responsibilities in this matter are ended. Yours now commence."

The jury retired for barely half an hour before finding Preeper not guilty. Feelings whipped up by the election and trial were still at a boiling point. "Murder him," someone shouted from the public gallery moments after the verdict was announced. Preeper, for his own safety, had to be spirited out of Province House by sheriff's constables.

* * *

"The verdict rendered will meet with a hearty response throughout the length and breadth of the land," *The Morning Chronicle* predicted. That was the Liberal view. The Conservative *British Colonist* termed the outcome a "whitewash." Charges and counter-charges flew in the press for weeks after the trial. *The Morning Chronicle* accused the attorney general's son of trying to counsel a witness to commit perjury. In the *Colonist*, Preeper's acquittal was attributed to a "corrupt" grand jury and "a no less accommodating" trial jury. "They will long be remembered as men ... who have shewn that any crime may be perpetrated with impunity provided party interests are at stake."

But Preeper had been singled out, while the men who had instigated the riot – government employees dispatched to the polling station to disrupt the election – had escaped prosecution. Even a non-partisan jury could be excused, in the circumstances, for ignoring the letter of the law.

The man at the centre of the political storm was free for the first time in seven months. George Preeper lived out his life on the Guysborough Road, not far from Grand Lake, earning a reputation as an experienced hunting guide. "There are few sportsmen in the city who have not been to Preeper's shooting or fishing," the Halifax *Evening Mail* noted almost four decades after the trial. "The Guysborough road has the chief woodcock and partridge covers of the county, and not far from Preeper's are trout lakes."

George Preeper returned to the public spotlight in the summer of 1895, when he married a twenty-two-year-old woman named Johnson. The event made news not only because Preeper was old enough to be her grandfather – it was generally assumed he was already married. But, as one reporter put it, Preeper convinced a minister that "the woman with whom he had lived for years, and whom he had introduced as his wife, was no relation to him." Almost forty years after he was cleared of killing a man largely because he had backed the right political party, Preeper managed to talk his way out of a possible prosecution for bigamy.

Part V

Deadly Disasters

12

The Halifax Explosion's Fallout

Benjamin Russell was only half-dressed when an explosion shook his Halifax rooming house and shattered its windows. Other residents, convinced "a bomb from the sky" had exploded nearby, urged Russell to join them in the safety of the basement. But curiosity drew the sixty-eight-year-old to the front door.

He stood at the corner of Barrington and Morris streets and looked toward the city's North End. "A gently curving column of fire, of all the colours that fire can assume, was ascending from the region of the Dockyard," he marvelled, "spreading and becoming wider and wider as it rose in height."

It was shortly after nine on the morning of December 6, 1917, and Russell was a witness to the biggest human-made explosion before the atomic age. After colliding with the freighter *Imo* in Halifax Harbour, the French munitions ship *Mont-Blanc* had caught fire and blown up, killing and maiming thousands and levelling large sections of Halifax and Dartmouth.

Word spread that fires could ignite ammunition stockpiles at the Naval Dockyard, triggering a second blast. Russell joined

Flattened buildings and shattered railcars in Halifax's North End after the 1917 explosion, which killed almost 2,000 people. In the background is *Imo*, the freighter that collided with the munitions ship *Mont-Blanc*, beached on the opposite side of the harbour. (International Film Service Inc./McCord Museum MP-0000.173.2)

a stream of people walking southward, away from the cloud of smoke hanging over the city, to Point Pleasant Park. No one was sure what had happened, or how serious the explosion had been. "A congenial company collected in the Park," recalled Russell, a dapper man with a well-groomed white beard, "to whom the hours passed swiftly."

But it was not long before the scale of the disaster was driven home. Russell spent the evening looking for his brother, John, a waterfront official, finally finding him in the Victoria General Hospital. Luckily, he had suffered only minor injuries. The following morning he was back at the hospital, where he volunteered to look after the growing number of homeless children gathering there. The room set aside to house them was a mess; every window was smashed and snow covered the floor. Rolling up his sleeves, Russell bought a roll of rubber-coated fabric and nailed it over the windows. When a steamer arrived from Boston a few days later with clothing and emergency supplies, he ordered that the hallways of the city's main courthouse be used as a drop-off point, until the goods could be distributed to survivors. But in the months ahead, Russell would play a pivotal role in the aftermath of the explosion not as a repairman or a relief worker, but as a Supreme Court judge.

* * *

"There was no upheaval of nature on that awful day," *The Halifax Herald* soon told its shocked readers. "No enemy sent a shell hurtling into the city." Almost two thousand people had died; another nine thousand had been injured, many of them blinded by shards of glass blasted into their faces as windows imploded. But who was to blame? Who was responsible for the death and destruction visited on a city an ocean away from the battlefields of the First World War? The Canadian government launched an inquiry to get to the bottom of the disaster.

In the meantime, rumours were rampant that the explosion was the work of German saboteurs. On December 10 Halifax police rounded up and jailed residents of German descent. Anti-German hysteria gripped the crippled city. "So long as there are people in Halifax who remember this past week, or whose children remember it," the *Herald* predicted six days after the explosion, "so long will the name of Germany be a name for loathing and disgust." At one point the search for a scapegoat centred on Johan Johansen, a Norwegian and the helmsman of *Imo*, one of the ships involved in the collision. He had survived the explosion and the Halifax police, convinced that a letter found in his possession was written in German, arrested him. Johansen was soon freed, once it was determined that the writing was in Norwegian.

German saboteurs, real or imaginary, were not the only possible culprits. Suspicion also fell on the crew that had brought *Mont-Blanc*'s lethal cargo into Halifax. The munitions ship's thirty-eight-year-old French skipper, Captain Aimé Le Medec, and local pilot Frank Mackey, forty-five, had fled the burning ship before it

"Is a man to be sent to the penitentiary for making a mistake?" asked Justice Benjamin Russell, who ignored press and public demands to find scapegoats for the explosion. (Author collection)

exploded. For many, their survival in the face of such widespread destruction confirmed their guilt. Fingers were also pointed at the official who had permitted *Mont-Blanc* to enter the harbour, Commander Frederick Evans Wyatt. As chief examining officer for the Port of Halifax, Wyatt was responsible for monitoring the movements of all vessels entering and leaving Halifax.

The commission of inquiry began its work a week after the explosion in the courthouse on Spring Garden Road, the building Justice Russell had requisitioned to store relief supplies. The chairman was his Supreme Court colleague Justice Arthur Drysdale, a former attorney general. At sixty, Justice Drysdale was in his tenth year on the bench. From the start, writer Michael J. Bird pointed out in his account of the explosion, *The Town That Died*, the judge "showed a bias in favour of the *Imo*."

Questioning witnesses called before the commission were two of the ablest lawyers in the city. Humphrey Mellish, who appeared for the owners of *Mont-Blanc*, was the "acknowledged leader" of the Nova Scotia bar, according to one observer. "His knowledge of the law is almost an institution." On the opposing side was C.J. Burchell, acting for *Imo*'s owners. "He was to prove, throughout the inquiry, capable of the most ruthless courtroom tactics and was constantly to attack and browbeat witnesses," noted Bird.

The first witnesses were Le Medec and Mackey. They agreed on the events leading up to the collision, testifying that *Mont-Blanc* had entered the harbour and steamed along the Dartmouth side of the harbour, in keeping with the rules of navigation. In the narrowest section of the harbour, with little room to manoeuvre, they had encountered the outbound *Imo*. Despite a frantic exchange of whistle signals to announce course adjustments and avoid a collision, *Imo* had sliced into the hold of *Mont-Blanc*, setting its powder-keg cargo ablaze.

On cross-examination, Burchell established that the ship was not flying a red warning flag, a precaution Le Medec insisted was required only during the loading or unloading of explosives. *Imo*'s lawyer also asked about the language barrier between the pilot and the captain. "We spoke mostly in signs," Le Medec admitted, testifying through an interpreter, but "everything was clear between us." Burchell took a more aggressive stance in questioning Mackey, accusing the pilot of lying to the court and of being a heavy drinker. But Mackey, a pilot with twenty-four years' experience and an accident-free record prior to the collision, denied the accusations.

Survivors from *Imo*, including helmsman Johansen, gave a conflicting version of events leading up to the collision. *Imo* altered its course to avoid an incoming American steamer, then was forced to steer even closer to the Dartmouth shore by a tugboat towing barges. *Mont-Blanc* was sighted and appeared to be passing at a safe distance when it veered across *Imo*'s path.

But *Imo* should not have been heading out to sea in the first place. Commander Wyatt testified he had not authorized the ship to leave its anchorage. Although pilots were supposed to keep him informed of vessel arrivals and departures, he admitted this was not always done. Experienced pilots were in short supply to cope with the port's heavy wartime traffic, and no one could afford to crack down on those who broke the rules.

The commission closed its hearings on January 28, 1918. A week later Drysdale delivered his findings. Despite the conflicting evidence, he laid the blame for the collision squarely on *Mont-Blanc*. That ship alone, he concluded, had caused the collision by violating the rules of the road. Mackey was guilty of "gross negligence" and the judge recommended he be dismissed as a pilot and prosecuted under the criminal law. Le Medec likewise should have his master's licence cancelled and be "dealt with according to the law of his country." Both men were also rapped for "neglect of the public safety" by not warning the city's inhabitants of the impending explosion. Wyatt, Drysdale concluded, had neglected his duty to monitor vessel movements in the harbour.

Nova Scotia's attorney general, Orlando T. Daniels, had already issued a warrant for the arrest of the *Mont-Blanc*'s captain and pilot on a charge of manslaughter. William Hayes, the *Imo*'s pilot, who had died in the explosion, was named as the specific victim of the alleged homicide. Mackey, who was sitting in the courtroom as Drysdale read his decision, was arrested as he left the courthouse. Le Medec was picked up a short time later as he walked through downtown Halifax. The pair were arraigned and ordered detained unless they could post substantial bail – $10,000 for the captain, $6,000 for the pilot.

*   *   *

The *Herald* wholeheartedly endorsed the commission's ruling. "There are no ambiguities, there is no pussyfooting ... the conclusions are concisely stated in clear cut concrete language with a decisiveness and fearlessness that everyone expected from Justice Drysdale." But the arrests only whetted the paper's appetite for more. "*The Halifax Herald* also demands the immediate arrest of Commander Wyatt so that he can be placed on trial for his responsibility in the frightful catastrophe."

The call was heeded on February 5, the day the editorial appeared. Under instructions from the attorney general, police arrested Wyatt at his Edward Street home and brought him to court in time for the preliminary hearing for Le Medec and Mackey. After Wyatt's bail was set at $6,000, a magistrate began hearing evidence against the trio in the grand jury room of the courthouse. The setting was appropriate – the room still showed signs of damage from the explosion two months earlier. Cracked plaster and a boarded-up window "combined to make up a dismal setting for one of the most important chapters in a great tragedy," wrote a *Herald* reporter with a flair for melodrama.

Prosecuting the case was Andrew Cluney. Walter J. O'Hearn, a thirty-eight-year-old Halifax lawyer, appeared for Mackey while Wyatt chose to watch the proceedings without counsel. Mellish acted for the *Mont-Blanc*'s captain on the opening day of the preliminary hearing, a Friday, but was appointed to the Supreme Court over the weekend. Hector McInnis, Mellish's former law partner, picked up Le Medec's case.

The preliminary hearing was brief. Most testimony came from *Imo*'s crew but one witness, not heard by the commission of inquiry, shed new light on the collision. The captain of a tug berthed at the naval dockyard testified that *Imo* caused the collision by changing course at the last minute. Despite the new evidence, all three men were ordered to stand trial before the Supreme Court.

The prosecution of the *Mont-Blanc*'s captain and pilot, however, came to a swift end. O'Hearn filed a motion of habeas corpus with the Supreme Court demanding the release of Mackey, who had been unable to raise bail money and remained in custody. The motion came before Justice Benjamin Russell, who believed there was no basis for the manslaughter allegation.

"It seemed to me that, so far from being negligent or careless ... the defendant had taken every possible care to prevent the collision which was about to be caused by the conduct of the *Imo*," the judge would recall in his memoirs, displaying the same compassion he had displayed in the days following the explosion. "It surely cannot have been manslaughter for a defendant to have done what was best in his judgment to prevent an impending accident even if, in spite of his best efforts, the struggle was unsuccessful."

Rejecting the findings of Justice Drysdale, a judge three years his junior on the bench, Justice Russell not only ordered Mackey's release – he ruled there was no basis for the criminal charges against either the pilot or Le Medec.

On March 19, Wyatt's case went to a grand jury empanelled to decide if there was sufficient evidence to warrant a trial. Justice Russell, again on the bench, assured them that the evidence against Wyatt "fell short of the requirements for an indictment for manslaughter." Well aware of the community's thirst for revenge – someone speaking to one of his sons, unaware of the relationship, had ventured the opinion that he should be castrated for freeing the captain and pilot – he seized the opportunity to explain his rationale. Mackey should not be held criminally negligent for an error in judgment made "under circumstances in which the most

careful and painstaking navigator could easily have been misled."
As for Le Medec, it would have been "absurd" to hold him criminally responsible because the ship, once in the harbour, was in the hands of the pilot.

"When a great calamity such as that which has visited this city occurs," he continued in his instructions to Wyatt's grand jury, "there is a very natural and pardonable disposition ... to demand vengeance and seek to hold somebody criminally responsible." With Mackey and Le Medec no longer facing prosecution, he noted, "it is quite possible that the injured feelings of the community should be concentrated upon the naval official," Wyatt.

He was right. Ignoring his instructions to throw out the case, the twenty-four-member grand jury returned an indictment sending Wyatt to trial. "To suppose that he had anything in the world to do with the disaster was an utterly lunatic notion," Justice Russell later complained. "It was simply nonsensical." The grand jury's decision "was symptomatic of the condition of the common feeling."

Prosecutor Cluney, emboldened by the outcome, launched an appeal to reinstate the charges against Mackey and Le Medec. Three members of the four-judge panel that heard the appeal upheld Justice Russell's decision. Not surprisingly, Justice Drysdale was the lone voice in dissent.

Cluney refused to give up. He was back in court on April 9, this time seeking a fresh indictment to bring Mackey before a grand jury. But the prosecutor was up against a brick wall in the form of Justice Russell. O'Hearn was first on his feet, objecting to the Crown's procedure and charging there was "an element of persecution" in the pursuit of Mackey. But Cluney contended he had fresh evidence bearing on the way the *Mont-Blanc* was navigated.

"Showing the pilot made a mistake?" Justice Russell snapped. "Do we not all make mistakes? Is a man to be sent to the penitentiary for making a mistake?" He dismissed the prosecution's motion as "an absolute absurdity." He likened Mackey's position to that of a surgeon losing a patient on the operating table, then having other doctors rule his actions "ill-advised" after an autopsy and leisurely study. He invited members of the public to put themselves in the pilot's shoes. "Would they not think that they had already suffered sufficiently without being indicted as criminals for what at the very worst was an error in judgment?"

All that remained was Wyatt's trial on April 17. It lasted less than a day and the evidence, despite Cluney's promise, shed no new light on the collision. Justice Russell, once again on the bench, told the twelve-man trial jury there was "nothing in the eyes of the law" to justify a manslaughter charge. These jurors heeded his instructions and acquitted Wyatt after a few minutes of deliberation. The prosecution did not appeal.

* * *

The civil courts also failed to assign legal blame for the disaster. In Admiralty Court, Justice Drysdale – echoing the findings of his earlier inquiry – ruled that *Mont-Blanc* had been at fault and awarded $2 million in damages to *Imo*'s owners. But he was ultimately overruled by the Supreme Court of Canada, which concluded the ships were equally liable for the collision.

"WHO IS GUILTY," demanded a *Herald* editorial the day after Wyatt's acquittal. "It now seems as if the whole matter is to be forgotten; that all the investigation has been in vain and that the responsibility for what was undoubtedly one of the most ghastly blunders the world has ever known, is never going to be fixed."

Mackey, suspended in the wake of the commission's findings, was eventually reinstated as a pilot. Le Medec continued to command vessels for *Mont-Blanc*'s owners until 1922, and retired in 1931. Wyatt, although cleared of criminal charges, was transferred from Halifax to a less sensitive post. And Justice Russell, who had worked tirelessly to prevent the three men from taking the fall for the explosion, retired from the bench in 1924, at age seventy-five. He made one last defence of his rulings on the explosion cases in his autobiography published in 1932, three years before his death.

QUEEN HOTEL, HALIFAX, N. S.

The Queen Hotel on Hollis Street, once one of the finest in Halifax and a favourite of politicians in town for sittings of the Legislature, fell on hard times during the Depression. (Author collection)

13

Inferno at the Queen Hotel

Ted Mitchell had no idea what woke him the winter morning Halifax's Queen Hotel burned to the ground. Smoke was coming into his room through the transom window over the door. "There was a roar, I didn't know what it was, in the hallway," he recalled. "I had sense enough to keep the door closed and go to the window."

He was trapped, three stories up. Fire was rapidly engulfing the hotel, fire trucks were pulling up, and people were screaming for help as firefighters frantically tried to reach them with ladders. Mitchell, a forty-nine-year-old salesman, either jumped or fell. "I was on the window sill, that's the last thing I remember 'til I came to on the ground." He was lying on the pavement on the waterfront side of the hotel, unable to move.

"You're all right now, you're out of the fire," said one of the men who came to his aid. He had broken both legs and an arm in the fall. Mitchell was carried to a store on Lower Water Street, where the proprietor looked after him. "I wanted a drink of water and the old lady was very kind and very much concerned about the situation, so she gave me a drink of milk. The next thing was, police cars came along, and I remember someone saying: 'You better take this fellow, he's hurt pretty bad.'" Mitchell was put in the back seat of a cruiser and rushed to Victoria General Hospital. It would be fourteen months before he recovered and walked out the hospital's doors.

He had been lucky to escape with his life. Twenty-eight people died on the morning of March 2, 1939. Out of almost ninety guests and employees in the hotel at the time of the fire, another nineteen were injured, suffering burns, cuts, and broken bones. The hotel and two adjoining buildings were razed, causing an estimated $800,000 damage. The Queen Hotel fire was Halifax's worst in half a century, and the worst disaster to befall the city since the explosion of 1917.

"Hollis Street looked as if it had been ripped by a tornado," *The Halifax Herald* reported the morning after the tragedy. "Debris littered the street, and all lanes of traffic were blocked by fire apparatus ... The skeleton walls of the once-famous hotel were reminiscent of scenes in battle-scarred France."

The inferno raised questions about fire safety in hotels, schools, theatres, and public buildings across Nova Scotia, and revealed shocking lapses in the enforcement of fire regulations. A public inquiry and a royal commission were set up to probe the disaster, culminating in the prosecution of the hotel's owner in the criminal courts on a charge of willfully causing the fatal fire.

* * *

In its heyday, the Queen was one of Halifax's top hotels. The site on the east side of Hollis Street, between Sackville and Salter streets, was first occupied by the International Hotel, which burned down in the 1870s without loss of life. The hotel was rebuilt and purchased in 1886 by A.B. Sheraton, a New Brunswick businessman who had no experience in the hotel trade. Sheraton, described as "enterprising and impulsive," resolved to turn the rather dilapidated premises into a first-class hotel. By 1890 he had

"Hollis Street looked as if it had been ripped by a tornado," *The Halifax Herald* reported in the aftermath of the 1939 fire that killed 28 people. A section of the hotel collapsed into the street. (Nova Scotia Archives No. 1995-370/6)

spent more than $70,000 to renovate and buy new furniture for the renamed Queen, but he was mired in debt. Sheraton's backers foreclosed, and after a messy court battle had him ejected from the premises. The shareholders leased the hotel to J.P. Fairbanks, who bought the property in 1901.

The Queen and its Hollis Street neighbour, the Halifax Hotel, were the luxury hotels of their time. Hollis Street was the heart of Halifax's business district, only a short walk from the waterfront that was the lifeblood of a city built on overseas trade. The Queen boasted two large, mirror-lined dining rooms for meetings and luncheons. A rooftop garden, shaded by awnings, offered a view of the harbour and a cool oasis in the summer. Located only two blocks south of Province House, it was a popular haunt for politicians in town for sittings of the legislature. It was widely believed, author Thomas Raddall noted in his chronicle of Halifax's history, *Warden of the North*, that more government business was transacted at the Queen than in Province House itself.

Renovations and expansion transformed the Queen into a rambling, ninety-three-room hotel with three distinct sections. The lobby, elevators, newsstand, and hotel offices were in the original, five-storey wooden structure. On the south side was an addition built in 1908 of concrete, with offices at street level and bedrooms on the upper floors. At the rear, stretching towards the harbour as far as Upper Water Street, was a section containing the kitchen, dining rooms, furnace room, and three more floors of bedrooms.

By 1930, the once posh Queen was past its prime. A building permit was obtained that year to carry out renovations, but the work was never done. The Depression was no time to pump scarce cash into the upkeep of a hotel. Even though the Queen was beginning to show its age, it still attracted prominent guests. R.T. Caldwell, the former Tory MLA for Kings County and a member of the province's board of censors, was a permanent resident. So was Arthur DeWitt Foster, another Annapolis Valley Tory who had caused a scandal during the First World War by acting as the federal Militia Department's purchasing agent for horses while sitting as a government Member of Parliament. In all, about forty-five people called the Queen home.

Ted Mitchell lived in Bridgewater and travelled the province selling tinned milk. "I always stayed at the Queen Hotel when I was working in the city," he recalled. It was "a good old hotel under the conditions," and seemed as safe as any he stayed in while on the road.

In June 1936, Halifax businessman John Simon paid a paltry $17,500 for the Queen. The price was so good, he bought the property without bothering to inspect its condition. "I was satisfied, knowing the property," he explained. Simon knew a good buy when he saw one. After arriving in the city in 1896 at age twenty, he had built a successful firm dealing in scrap metal, then diversified into shipping on a modest scale. He operated several small vessels under the imposing name Hochelaga Shipping and Towing Company; the flagship of the fleet was *Hochelaga*, a cargo and passenger boat with a regular run between Pictou, Nova Scotia, and Prince Edward Island. He also dabbled in real estate, and that brought him to the Queen.

Like Sheraton before him, Simon had no experience running a hotel. And he had trouble finding someone who did, going through four managers in less than three years. His son, Sydney, and a daughter, Ida, helped out, but day-to-day decisions such as staffing and minor purchases were left up to the manager. Simon later insisted he had pumped $30,000 into repairing the hotel by 1939, but the claim seems unlikely; the building and furniture combined were insured for only $33,000. With business slow everywhere, it was a time for cost-cutting, not capital outlays. One of Simon's first acts as president of the Queen Hotel Company Limited was to trim the staff from about forty to twenty-nine, including cutting the night shift from four employees to two. He also trimmed salaries. But a smaller payroll did little to improve the bottom line; the hotel consistently operated in the red.

* * *

Wednesday, March 1, 1939. This was the day John Desmond would rid himself of Victor Bouffard. Desmond, an officious manager who had been in charge at the Queen Hotel for a number of months, was fed up with Bouffard's drinking on duty. As one of the hotel's firemen, Bouffard was responsible for stoking the furnace with coal and patrolling the building on the night shift, but most of the time, he was drunk. "Dirty drunk," Desmond called it.

The dismissal had been cleared with the owner. After all, Bouffard had come to the Queen after working as a deckhand on one of Simon's boats, and knew the boss. When Bouffard picked up his pay envelope that afternoon, inside was a note giving him two-weeks' notice.

"I started to celebrate," recalled Bouffard, a heavy-set man with a hook nose and a full head of black hair. He bought two bottles of scotch, downed one, went to a restaurant for a meal, and then drank the other. About nine in the evening, he rolled into the lobby of the Queen and gave Desmond a piece of his mind.

"If I'm out of a job, then there's going to be a lot more looking for a job tomorrow," he threatened, then babbled something about seeing Desmond in the penitentiary "and I'll laugh at you." Desmond told Bouffard to clear out of the hotel.

Bouffard staggered off, polished off a third bottle of liquor, and returned to the hotel after Desmond went to bed. The night desk clerk, Eddie Weaver, let him stay, fearing Bouffard "might start a row." Besides, Weaver could use the help. The night clerk was severely overworked: he was supposed to man the desk and switchboard, operate the elevator, clean the lobby, patrol the building, and duck out for food for the guests. Despite Bouffard's condition, when he offered to run the elevator, Weaver agreed.

About two in the morning, a guest who had lived at the hotel for twenty years, Harvey Putman, called the switchboard. He thought he smelled smoke. Weaver roused Desmond and they traced the smoke to a janitor's closet on the second floor of the hotel's rear section, four floors above the furnace room. Inside, they found a newspaper burning in a garbage can. Weaver pulled the can into the hall and used an extinguisher to douse the flames.

The closet wall had been scorched, but there was no other damage. The fire had obviously been set – burnt matches were lying on the floor.

Desmond had a good idea who the culprit might be, and found Bouffard passed out in a chair in the lobby. Despite his suspicions, the manager left Bouffard there and did not report the incident to the fire department. Desmond went back to his room in the hotel to sleep. But the fire had rattled Weaver, who stepped up his patrols of the building to every half-hour. "I was just uneasy," he explained. So was the guest who had smelled smoke. Putman got dressed and hung around the lobby for almost an hour before returning to his room.

A poker game in Room 166 broke up about three-thirty in the morning and the four players headed for bed. Weaver, the only one left awake in the building, went into the hotel office about five-thirty to write a letter. A few minutes later, Bouffard woke up in the lobby, "feeling kind of seedy," as he put it. He had no recollection of his run-in with Desmond, or how he had ended up sleeping in the lobby. Thirsty and hungover, he bought a bottle of ginger ale from Weaver and headed downstairs to the furnace room to pick up his belongings.

He smelled smoke in the stairwell. Just the furnace, he thought. But when he passed the furnace room, he saw no smoke. "That struck me as funny," Bouffard recalled. He went into the next room and woke up the day fireman, Arthur Caldwell, then headed upstairs to see where the smoke was coming from. He got as far as the landing. The floor between the furnace room and the lobby was filled with smoke and Bouffard could see flames licking at the walls. Caldwell was getting dressed as Bouffard burst into his room.

"Great God!" he shouted. "Get up. There's a fire!" By now the furnace room was thick with smoke. Caldwell went inside, turned off the boilers to prevent an explosion, and woke up other staff members who lived at the rear of the hotel. He and Bouffard escaped by breaking a window overlooking an alley.

Upstairs, headwaitress Sophie Martell had gone to the lobby

to check the guest list, to find out how many people to expect for breakfast. It was about twenty minutes past six. As she turned to go back to the dining room, smoke began billowing into the lobby. "It was so thick I couldn't get through," she said. Weaver stuck his head out of the hotel office. "Oh God, Sophie!" he yelled. "A fire!" He ran to the switchboard, called the fire department, then tried to awaken guests by calling their rooms. He got through to one man before the heavy smoke drove him out of the building.

Charles Lynch, a twenty-year-old cub reporter for Halifax's sister papers, the *Herald* and *Mail*, was walking past the hotel after working the night shift. The air was cold but there was no snow – a typical late-winter day in Halifax. Suddenly a curtain of fire swept out of the front of the hotel, shattering the lobby's large windows.

The first fire trucks were on the scene within minutes, but the fire spread with deadly speed. The elevator shaft was not fireproof, giving the flames a path to the upper floors. Flames and smoke quickly turned upstairs hallways into deathtraps. People unable to flee their rooms on the upper floors stood at their windows, screaming for help. Some tried to climb down knotted bedsheets. Below, firefighters dropped their hoses and concentrated on putting up ladders to rescue them. A tangle of overhead power lines and trolley cables hampered their efforts, and not even the fire department's lone aerial ladder could reach the top floor.

Heroes were made that morning. Clyde MacIntosh, the Queen's daytime desk clerk, awoke in his fourth-floor room about six-thirty, choking on smoke. Jumping onto the fire escape outside his window, he began pounding on windows to wake guests. He helped nine people down the fire escape, the last an unconscious man he carried over his shoulders to safety. The iron rungs on the fire escape were so hot they were burning his feet, but MacIntosh scurried back up. He reached the third floor but was overcome by smoke and toppled onto the pavement below. Incredibly, he was not seriously injured.

Other scenes were etched forever on the memories of guests and rescuers alike. Robert Murray, the former sheriff of Cumberland County, made it to the street, but ran back into the burning building to save his wife. Both perished. One woman grabbed at a ladder, missed, and clung to a window ledge as firefighters used their hoses to beat back the flames. Two firefighters climbed the ladder and managed to put a rope under her arms just as she lost consciousness.

About a dozen people jumped to the roof of the hotel's rear section, but fell to their deaths when it collapsed into the inferno below. A man named Elliff dropped his two young children into a life net thirty feet below. "It was a terrible feeling," he confessed later, "but it was the only thing to do." The children were unharmed. One firefighter climbed through a window and saw the figure of a woman kneeling in prayer, silhouetted against the flames. A rush of searing heat drove him back to the window before he could reach her.

By mid-morning it was all over. Newsman Lynch, who had stood transfixed as the drama unfolded in front of him, rushed back to his office to help get out an extra of the afternoon paper. It was a scoop. The fire cut power lines to the offices of the Halifax *Star*, and the rival afternoon paper was unable to run its presses.

Initial reports put the death toll as high as fifty, but that number was reduced to twenty-eight after the hotel register was recovered from a safe in the ruins. The dead included former politicians R.T. Caldwell and Arthur DeWitt Foster, retired provincial engineer Rod McColl, and the Cuban consul. Many of the bodies were so badly burned they could only be identified through dental records. The remains of ten people were never identified.

The legislature adjourned for the day out of respect for the dead, after Premier Angus L. Macdonald moved a resolution of sympathy for the victims and their families. Telegrams of condolence poured in as news of the disaster flashed around the globe. One arrived from King George VI, who assured the people of

Halifax that the British government joined "in the general expression of sympathy which this catastrophe will evoke throughout the entire country."

There were loud demands for an investigation. "Let it be probed to the bottom," proclaimed a front-page editorial in the Halifax *Evening Mail*. "There must be a full and far-reaching investigation," demanded the New Glasgow *Evening News*, adding that "it will likely be found that many other buildings used for the same purpose throughout the province are equally dangerous." Opposition Leader P.C. Black called on the provincial government to launch an inquiry. "I have been informed ... that there may not have been adequate fire escape protection in the burned hotel," he charged.

There would be two public inquiries. The fire marshal opened an investigation on March 6. Within days, the government appointed a royal commission, headed by Justice M.B. Archibald of the Supreme Court, with a mandate to probe the Queen Hotel disaster and the state of fire prevention in the province.

* * *

Testimony of survivors and hotel staff revealed that the Queen broke virtually every fire regulation on the books. The rooms were not fitted with ropes, which guests could use to lower themselves to the ground. There was no fire alarm to awaken them. The iron fire escapes had wooden landings that had quickly burned away. There were no signs in the rooms to show the direction to the fire escapes and, besides, access was through private rooms and behind locked doors. None of the staff members had been told what to do in case of a fire. The only redeeming feature was the presence of fire extinguishers, two to a floor, all apparently in working order.

It became increasingly obvious that responsibility for the shocking safety lapses lay with one man: John Simon. "From the day I stepped into the hotel, I did everything possible" to prevent a fire, the owner claimed during one of the inquiries. "I always employed first class mechanics on that kind of work." But when pressed, the only example Simon could offer was hiring a man to chip rust from the fire escapes and paint them.

Simon had found it easy to ignore safety laws because none were enforced. Inspecting Nova Scotia's hotels, it turned out, was the responsibility of the factories inspector, Phillip Ring. But he only visited a premises when he received a complaint. Ring had inspected all Halifax hotels in 1937 at the request of the provincial minister of labour. Violations of fire safety laws were noted in writing, but there was no follow-up to see if hotelkeepers corrected the problems.

Ring's dealings with the Queen illustrated the danger of this hands-off policy. He inspected the hotel in March 1937 and ordered four immediate steps be taken to conform with safety laws: install ropes in each room; repair handrails on the fire escapes; post signs in the hallways to show the location of fire escapes; and post similar notices in each room. Ring sent a letter to hotel management outlining the deficiencies but he never returned to ensure his instructions were carried out. Asked why he did not prosecute, Ring offered a weak explanation: the hotel's manager at the time, E.E. Amirault, had been a friend from childhood and he had trusted him to comply with the letter.

Amirault testified he had personally read the letter to Simon, who had directed his former manager to fix the handrails and to ignore the other instructions. Amirault's version of events was corroborated by the handyman who repaired the fire escapes. Simon, for his part, denied any knowledge of the letter.

Hearings continued into the late spring of 1939, but reports of the testimony were often swept off the front pages by the bleak news of a world on the brink of a second world war. Justice Archibald delivered the royal commission's report in November, coming down hard on fire safety officials. The legislation was sound, he said; what was needed was a vigorous, coordinated effort to enforce those laws. He called for a revamped fire marshal's office, directly responsible to the government and armed with more power to enforce fire regulations. As for the Halifax Fire Department, the judge reported that it was undermanned and its equipment was outdated and inadequate. The aerial ladder, dating from 1919, was so rickety the fire chief had warned his men that they used it at their own risk.

The judge could not determine from the evidence the exact cause of the fire. It had apparently started just above the furnace room, possibly where unprotected pipes from the furnace came too close to the wooden ceiling. Another suggestion was that an ember from the early-morning fire in the janitor's closet had dropped down the wall, and smouldered for several hours before starting a new fire. The report made no mention of Bouffard's threat or the suspicion that he had set that earlier fire. "There is nothing in the evidence to justify the conclusion that the fire was deliberately set," the judge wrote.

But Justice Archibald left no doubt who was responsible for the deaths. The judge was satisfied the owner had known of the 1937 letter outlining safety measures to be taken. "The person responsible for this non-compliance with the inspector's requirements," he announced, "was John Simon."

Halifax police had begun questioning hotel staff, including Vic Bouffard, while firefighters were still pouring water over the smouldering ruins. Little more than two weeks after Justice Archibald tendered his report, a charge of willfully causing a fire through negligence was laid against the sixty-three-year-old scrap dealer-turned-hotelkeeper. It was believed to be the first prosecution in Canada under a section of the Criminal Code, introduced in 1919, that made owners of burned buildings criminally responsible for causing a fire if they "failed to obey the requirements of any law intended to prevent fires," and if loss of life "would not have occurred if such law had been complied with." A conviction could bring up to five years in prison.

* * *

Simon's health was not good – he was ill at home at the time of the fire – and his preliminary hearing on the charge was adjourned several times because he was too sick to come to court. Finally, in October 1940, with all the evidence in, he was ordered to stand trial. The case went before the County Court in January 1941. The judge was Robert H. Murray, an outspoken, progressive-minded former Crown prosecutor. "A kindly soul – a friend of humanity who was known for his keen sense of humour and conversant with the problems that beset mankind," recalled one Halifax lawyer who knew him well.

The events leading up to the fire had been well-sifted during previous inquiries, so the prosecution concentrated on the deaths of three guests in making its case against Simon. They included John Johnson, who was passing through Halifax after refereeing a hockey game and had checked into the Queen just hours before the fire broke out. The three victims had been in the part of the building farthest from the area where the fire started, making them the most likely to have escaped if proper fire safety equipment had been installed.

Murray mulled over the evidence for two weeks before handing down his ruling. He took a dim view of how Simon had run his business. "It is safe to say that, like many other hotels in the province, the company had not conformed to the laws made for the safeguarding of guests from the hazards of fire," he said when court reconvened on January 30, 1941. "No doubt the protection of dollars rather than that of human life received the greatest consideration. ... The hotel was run at a comparatively heavy loss which was not an inspiration to the company to do anything further for the protection of the guests."

With those preliminary thoughts out of his system, Murray turned to the law. The prosecution had established that Simon had been negligent in not complying with fire safety laws, but the section required proof that the fire and the deaths it caused "would not have occurred" if he had done so. Would ropes in the rooms, a central fire alarm, and signs in the rooms and hallways showing the location of fire escapes have saved Johnson and the others? Murray thought many of the twenty-eight victims would probably have been awakened by an alarm and escaped, "but in view of the criminal law a probability is not sufficient to convict. If the law read 'the loss of life might not have occurred' I may have been at liberty to draw a convincing inference." The case turned on a single word. The judge, noting he had to give the accused the benefit of the doubt, found Simon not guilty.

* * *

Simon's troubles were far from over. He faced lawsuits from survivors and families of victims of the blaze; one action, seeking $5,600 in damages, was settled out of court for an undisclosed amount. He was also hauled back into court in April 1941, charged with breaching fire regulations by installing shingles that were not fire-resistant on a group of waterfront buildings. The prosecution reflected a new resolve on the part of inspectors, in the wake of the Queen Hotel tragedy, to enforce fire safety laws. But Simon was acquitted again, this time because he did not appear to own the buildings – he was still negotiating to buy them when the charge was laid.

Simon died in a Halifax nursing home in April 1966. He was ninety. Charles Lynch earned a ten-dollar bonus for his scoop on the fire, and went on to become one of Canada's best-known political pundits. The Queen Hotel site remained vacant until the Bank of Canada erected a new building there in the late 1950s. And Ted Mitchell, who lived to be 101, went back to selling milk. But his harrowing escape was not soon forgotten.

"I used to check every hotel I'd go to. I'd see if there was a rope in the room," he recalled with a chuckle about a year before his death in 1990. "I went into one hotel, and I won't mention the name, and I said, 'Ropes in good order?'"

The manager assured him they were, and pointed to the one in his room.

"So I picked it up and uncoiled it and dropped it out of the window. It went down about halfway to the pavement." Mitchell decided to spend the night in another hotel.

Part 6

Silent Witnesses

14

Tell-tale Chalk

It was settled – the two men would stay the night. Their host would hear of nothing else.

George Boutilier and his younger brother, John, had visited the homestead earlier that brisk March day in 1791, and George Frederick Eminaud was pleased to see they had returned. Eminaud, who had just turned seventy, lived with his wife and granddaughter on First Peninsula, near the South Shore settlement of Lunenburg. He appreciated having some male company. Besides, the Boutiliers were more like family than guests. The elder Boutilier was Eminaud's godson and namesake, so it was not surprising that the brothers, who lived a short distance inland at Northwest, often stopped by. But this would be their last visit. Heading to the barn through the darkness to fetch straw for his guests' bedding, Eminaud never suspected the real reason the Boutiliers had suddenly returned. They had needed some time to steel their courage for the work that lay ahead.

Eminaud, his arms wrapped around a bundle of straw, was almost to the house when his assailants struck with a hatchet and wooden clubs. He died on the spot. The Boutiliers headed inside and used the hatchet to kill Eminaud's wife. The granddaughter managed to crawl partway out of a window as she tried to escape. She was hauled back inside and hacked to death.

Eminaud was rumoured to have a stash of money and the Boutiliers sacked the house, greedily snatching everything they could find. They rifled Eminaud's pockets and helped themselves to the contents, even a piece of red chalk. Then the Boutiliers turned to the second phase of their plan. They dragged Eminaud's body inside and set fire to the house in hopes of destroying all evidence of the bloody deed. As flames consumed the house and the bodies of its occupants, the Boutiliers disappeared into the forest, headed eastward. To confuse their trackers, they strapped on their snowshoes backwards.

The glow of the fire could be seen from Lunenburg, but the house had burned to the ground by the time help arrived. Despite their efforts to erase evidence, the Boutiliers had been sloppy. Eminaud's bloodied hat was found on the ground beside two wooden clubs.

It took two days for the news to reach Halifax. For a triple murder committed so close to home, the crime commanded surprisingly little interest in the capital city's press. *The Weekly Chronicle* devoted a single paragraph to the Lunenburg murders, terming them a "horrid" and "unnatural deed." But the news, however sketchy, travelled faster than two men slogging through the bush and deep snow. Halifax County's sheriff was on the lookout and on March 24, five days after the murders, he arrested two men, newly arrived from Lunenburg, at a shanty north of the city. They were the Boutilier brothers.

They appeared before two justices of the peace the next day for questioning. "We do not learn that anything material transpired which tended to support the opinion of their guilt," the *Chronicle* informed its readers. "They are, however, still kept in custody." Unknown to the press, the authorities had come up with a compelling piece of evidence linking the Boutiliers to the crime. It was enough to charge the Boutiliers with murdering George Eminaud by inflicting "mortal strokes, wounds and bruises … with certain

"Wickedness often devises secret times and ways to perpetuate its evil designs," Chief Justice Thomas Strange told jurors at the 1791 murder trial of brothers George and John Boutilier. (Author collection)

large sticks and a tomahawk." There was no mention of Eminaud's wife and granddaughter in the indictment; the authorities may have held these possible charges in reserve, so they could be pursued if the two suspects were acquitted at trial. The brothers were imprisoned to await their day in court.

* * *

The last thing Nova Scotia's understaffed and much maligned judiciary needed was a major murder trial. The quality of the Supreme Court's judges had been under fire for years, with newcomers who had remained loyal to Britain during the American Revolution behind much of the criticism. Some of these Loyalist refugees were eager to claim Nova Scotia judicial posts for themselves.

When Chief Justice Bryan Finucane died in 1785, British authorities were slow to fill the vacancy. That left two assistant judges, Isaac Deschamps and James Brenton, to carry the court's entire workload. Until the 1830s, court rules required that two judges – the chief justice and one other – preside over trials. Justices Deschamps and Brenton were forced to handle every trial conducted in the far-flung communities springing up around the colony.

Neither was up to the task. Justice Deschamps was a former judge of the inferior court of common pleas, the lowest rung on the evolving colonial court structure. Although he had no formal legal training, he was appointed to the Supreme Court in 1770 and took over as chief justice upon Finucane's death. Justice Brenton at least had the legal credentials to be on the bench – he had been a lawyer in his native Rhode Island, and had served stints as Nova Scotia's solicitor general and attorney general. But even though he rose to the rank of the colony's chief law enforcement officer, Justice Brenton's legal expertise was suspect. One historian suggested he had been named to the Supreme Court in 1781 "for want of anyone better."

Dissatisfaction with the two judges erupted in 1787. The assembly, the colony's elected body, debated their track records in a rare secret session and emerged with a demand that Governor John Parr investigate their performance. The governor refused, but the complaints continued to fester. In 1790, the assembly voted to impeach both Deschamps and Brenton for "high crimes and misdemeanours." The impeachment motion was forwarded to London for a final decision, and it took another two years for the British government to decide that the pair should be allowed to keep their posts. Their shortcomings as judges, if any, were put down to "the frailty of human nature."

Steps were taken to beef up Nova Scotia's courts after the assembly went public with its criticisms. Deschamps was shunted aside as chief justice in the summer of 1788 in favour of Jeremy Pemberton. Here was someone with the law in his blood – grandson of a lord chief justice of England, Cambridge educated, a product of London's prestigious inns of court. But Pemberton lasted barely fourteen months as Nova Scotia's top judge. He resigned in the fall of 1789 due to ill health and died less than a year later. He was only forty-nine.

The British tried again, this time opting for someone even younger than Pemberton in an effort to put the colony's justice system back on track. Scottish-born Thomas Andrew Lumisden Strange was thirty-two when he was tapped to become Nova Scotia's sixth chief justice in 1789. The new top judge was an imposing figure but his chest-length judicial wig framed a surprisingly youthful face. He was far from comfortable in the courtroom. He enjoyed "a reputation as an excellent theoretical lawyer," noted Nova Scotia historian Brian Cuthbertson, "but he had little courtroom experience and he was somewhat unsure of himself." The trial of the Boutilier brothers would be his first major test.

* * *

In late April 1791, the Royal Navy schooner *Diligent* cast off from a Halifax wharf and took a southwesterly course once it cleared the harbour's mouth. On board were two passengers who had a date with the law in Lunenburg, George and John Boutilier. A few days later another navy vessel, the cutter *Alert*, followed bearing Chief Justice Strange and Justice Brenton. As chief justice, Strange would do all the talking once the murder trial got under way. And that was probably fine with Justice Brenton, who was still under the cloud of the assembly's impeachment resolution of the previous year.

Only one account of the three-day murder trial has survived, and hardly an unbiased one at that. Written by James Stewart, a Halifax lawyer and future judge who prosecuted the case, it provides few details of the evidence. A grand jury heard an outline of the prosecution's case on May 3 and ruled there was enough evidence to send the Boutiliers to trial. The following day Stewart delivered his opening address to the trial jury. The evidence against the two accused was "purely circumstantial," he admitted, "but after fullest consideration" it had "left in his mind a violent presumption that a murder had been committed." He was confident the jurors would draw the same "violent presumption" and conclude the Boutilier brothers were the killers.

Stewart called fifteen witnesses, including three members of the Boutilier family. He did not record how their testimony implicated their relatives. The most damning evidence came from Eminaud's son, who produced a broken piece of red chalk. The afternoon before the killings, he explained, his father had broken the chalk in half as they worked. The chalk fragment was then compared to a piece of chalk found in George Boutilier's pocket when he was arrested. The two pieces fitted together perfectly. To round out the Crown's case, two men swore they saw the Boutilier brothers crossing the ice of a nearby waterway as they fled the scene of the crime.

No evidence was called in their defence, and Stewart does not record whether they even had a lawyer to defend them. Then it was Chief Justice Strange's turn to enter the spotlight with his instructions to the jury. "If you have the smallest doubt, whether it regard the fact of the murders, the fact of the prisoners having been at the house or the design and end with which they might have been there," he explained, "it is my duty to tell you, and yours to mind what I say, that you ought to acquit them." He reminded them of a maxim at the heart of British law: "It is better any number of guilty persons escape punishment than that one innocent man suffer." But there was another option. "If you have no doubt," he continued, "but think that the finger of Providence has as plainly pointed the prisoners out doing this deed as if one had come and told you he saw them do it, in that case, and in that case only, you will find them guilty."

The chief justice then faced squarely the central issue of the trial – the prosecution's lack of direct evidence. "Wickedness often devises such secret times and ways to perpetrate its evil designs," he noted, "that if nothing but positive evidence could be received for juries to go upon in determining facts, crimes would forever go unpunished, and the condition of society be rendered most insecure."

Circumstantial evidence, he contended, could be "even more conclusive than a simple testimony of the fact itself." He used the example of a man seen fleeing a house carrying a bloody knife. The only other occupant of the house was found stabbed to death. The implication of guilt was inescapable.

Chief Justice Strange could have cited another compelling example – a piece of chalk belonging to a murder victim found in a suspect's pocket. It took the jurors an hour and a half to return a verdict of guilty against each man. The murder of Eminaud was "so black and dreadful" that it was "incapable of aggravation," the judge said in passing the death sentence. "Though from the present tribunal before which you stand you can receive nothing but strict and equal justice," he told the Boutiliers, "you are soon to appear before an almighty judge, whose unfathomable wisdom is able, by means incomprehensible to our narrow capacities, to reconcile justice with mercy."

Chief Justice Strange encouraged them to own up to their actions in the little time they had left. He ordered George and John Boutilier to hang within a week. John Boutilier, the younger of the two, confessed his role in the murders to a clergyman. The sentence was carried out in Lunenburg on May 9, 1791, at a spot dubbed Gallows Hill. "Their behaviour at the gallows was such as became men who were sensible of the horrid crime they had committed," one newspaper claimed. They were buried at Northwest, on the farm where they grew up.

Greed drove the Boutilier brothers to kill. It spurred them to steal everything in sight, even a piece of blood-red chalk – the shred of evidence that linked them beyond all doubt to the murders of the Eminauds.

15

The Leather Band

The sun was low in the morning sky when William Hussey approached the small, ramshackle cabin on John Clem's secluded farm in River Philip, Cumberland County. Hussey, his neighbour, had been promised some seed potatoes for spring planting, and he had come to collect.

Despite the early hour, Hussey thought it odd that the place looked deserted. After checking the barn, he climbed on the gunnel of a boat beached beside the cabin and peered through a window. "I heard heavy groaning and I thought they were asleep," he recalled. Then a woman's voice broke the morning stillness, crying out: "Oh Lord, have mercy on us."

Startled, Hussey sprang from his perch and barged through the unbolted door. He was confronted with a hideous sight. "I saw Clem lying before the fire on his bed, on the broad of his back, with his hands crossed on his breast. He was senseless," he said later. "His eye was bruised and swollen and the pillow covered in blood." Rushing to his side, Hussey shook Clem in an attempt to rouse him.

"I asked him who hurt him, but he made me no answer ... He snorted heavily and blood rushed from his mouth at every breath." Hussey moved on to the only other room in the cabin. There, lying amidst blood-spattered bedclothes, were Elizabeth Pipes, a widow who kept house for Clem, and her twelve-year-old daughter, Jane.

"I thought they were dead," was Hussey's first reaction. Both were clinging to life, but neither could tell Hussey what had happened. The mother, her forehead battered and slashed open, muttered something about a "nightmare."

Hussey looked up to see the shadow of a man against the wall. For a split second, he feared the assailant had returned to finish his work. He spun around, but was relieved to find himself standing face to face with another neighbour, John Winsby. Winsby, who was dropping off a bag of barley, was just as relieved to see that it was Hussey kneeling over the mangled victims.

There was little they could do. Clem died within minutes. Beside his bed were the splintered remains of a wooden chest, in which the farmer was reputed to keep a large amount of cash. Nothing of value remained. A bloodied axe was later found just outside the cabin. Hussey and Winsby had a good idea who had attacked the cabin's three occupants as they slept. Clem's hired hand, Maurice Doyle, was missing. Leaving Hussey at the cabin to comfort the two left alive, Winsby went to the nearest town, Pugwash, to summon a doctor and raise the alarm: a murderer was on the loose.

* * *

The date was June 28, 1838, and the citizens of Amherst were in a festive mood. It was the day of Queen Victoria's coronation, and her subjects in northern Nova Scotia's largest town were celebrating with parades and marching bands. But spirits dampened in the late afternoon when word arrived of the tragedy in River Philip, about thirty miles due east. Rumours began to fly that the suspect in the murder, Doyle, had passed through Amherst that morning and crossed the border into the neighbouring colony of New Brunswick.

A two-man posse mounted up to track him down. The law was represented by Joseph Avard, a justice of the peace who carried the warrant for Doyle's arrest. His companion was Asa Filmore, a River Philip resident who said he could identify their quarry.

After riding all night across the rough roads of backwoods New Brunswick, they pulled into the town of Sussex, a good one hundred miles from Amherst. Doyle was about to board a stage-coach bound for the city of Saint John when Filmore spotted him. Worried that Doyle might be armed, they took no chances. Filmore drew his pistol as Avard jumped Doyle and wrestled him to the ground. Caught off guard, Doyle offered no resistance as Avard tied him up with rope.

A search turned up a red-leather wallet containing £25 in bank notes, but no weapon. Told the reason for the arrest, Doyle seemed surprised.

"My God," he stammered. "Is Clem dead?"

"Yes," Filmore replied, "and you are the supposed murderer and must return and answer."

They took their prisoner to the nearest tavern, where Filmore began an impromptu interrogation. Asked where he got the money, Doyle said he had earned the large sum through "hard labour" in the United States. To explain his hasty exit from River Philip, Doyle told his captors he wanted to see his brother, who was about to sail from Saint John to the West Indies. When the questions turned to Clem, Doyle praised his former employer as "a clever man." He "paid me well," Doyle said, but Clem had told him on June 27 – the day before the murder – that his services were no longer needed. The last time he saw him, Doyle said, Clem was carrying a sack toward his farm and very much alive.

Avard and Filmore didn't believe a word of the story. Doyle was hauled back to Amherst, arraigned on a charge of murder, and tossed into jail to await a trial in the fall.

* * *

An early view of the town of Amherst, where Maurice Doyle stood trial for murder in 1838. (Canadian Illustrated News/Nova Scotia Archives N-7568)

"The annals of crime contain few such midnight acts of atrocity," a newspaper writer proclaimed when Clem's murder hit the pages of Halifax's *Acadian Recorder*. Although initial reports held out little hope for the recovery of Pipes and her daughter, both survived their ordeal.

The task of prosecuting Doyle fell to James F. Gray, a Halifax lawyer with about a dozen years at the bar. His most notable case, three years earlier, was the high-profile but failed prosecution of outspoken Halifax editor Joseph Howe for criminal libel. Gray had no eyewitnesses – the two survivors had no idea who had attacked them in their sleep. But the circumstantial evidence pointing to Doyle, coupled with his desperate attempt to flee, provided a good foundation for the prosecution's case. The challenge for Gray was to collect enough scraps of evidence to put the axe that felled Clem firmly in Doyle's hands.

The trial opened on September 25, 1838, to a full house. "At an early hour of the morning the streets of Amherst were crowded with persons thronging in from the country to witness the trial," noted one observer on the scene. "It was with some difficulty that a passage for the chief justice and the officers of the court could be made through the mass of men at the door of the courthouse."

The judge who had to elbow his way into the courthouse was Chief Justice Brenton Halliburton. "A small, delicate, light complexioned man," in the words of one spectator, Halliburton hardly fit in among the broad-shouldered farmers and shipbuilders who called Amherst home. And he would have been just as happy to have remained in the cultured surroundings of Halifax; he confessed to friends that he loathed travelling around the countryside to conduct trials. A judge for half of his sixty-three years, he was in his fifth year as the colony's top judge. Of his legal knowledge, one lawyer who appeared before him offered the backhanded compliment that it "was not very extensive, but like his wine it was of the best quality."

Doyle was brought into the courtroom, manacled and surrounded by a bevy of guards carrying tip staves – ceremonial, metal-tipped staffs – identifying them as sheriff's officers. On the chief justice's orders, the leg irons were removed once Doyle took his place in the prisoner's dock.

Doyle, only twenty-four, was a Cape Bretoner by birth who had taken odd jobs as a labourer in the River Philip area for about a year before Clem's death. He looked the part of a murderer, at least in the eyes of the newspaper reporters covering the trial. "A strong built, muscular man with large coarse features, dark hair and eyes, shaggy eyebrows and a down look," wrote the correspondent for the Halifax-based *Novascotian*. The whole package was a "mixture of brutality, ignorance and low cunning." The *Acadian Recorder*'s reporter in Amherst was just as uncharitable, stating bluntly: "His visage is repulsive." In an era when it was commonly believed that people who looked like criminals *were* criminals, Doyle's appearance alone may have been enough to convince a jury he was the killer.

Gray outlined the prosecution's case in a lengthy, at times eloquent opening speech. He cautioned the jurors that even though some details of the case had been widely circulated through the newspapers and the local rumour mill, "every feeling of excitement must be banished" from their minds. There could be no doubt this was a case of murder, not the less serious crime of manslaughter – an unintentional or provoked killing. "Blows from an axe had rained down on three people as they slept, and one had died from his wounds. Whoever committed the crime was, in law and in fact, a murderer," Gray asserted. The jury had only one issue to decide: Was Doyle that murderer?

"The testimony is but circumstantial," Gray continued, but this was not uncommon. "The man who meditates a murderous deed, chooses not the broad daylight for the perpetration of his crime; he seeks for darkness and secrecy … his steps are silent and unseen." The prosecutor assured the jury he could trace Doyle's movements over the course of two days, from the time of the offence to his sudden, suspicious flight into New Brunswick. He would show that Doyle had spun a web of lies to cover his tracks. And he would present the evidence needed to link Maurice Doyle to the brutal murder of John Clem.

* * *

Cumberland County's coroner, George Bayman, was the first witness. He left little to the jury's imagination, presenting the axe, stained with dark patches of dried blood, found outside Clem's cabin. Hussey and Winsby followed, describing their discovery of the three victims. Winsby, eager to explain why he had been at Clem's cabin so early in the morning, recalled how Clem had stopped by the day before his death, June 27, exhausted from carrying a bag of barley for several miles. Clem had left the sack at Winsby's house and rowed across the river to his cabin.

Winsby had delivered the barley the next morning, only to find his friend near death. When questioning was turned over to the defence, Doyle's lawyer did him no favours. Charles Halliburton was a young attorney who had been practising in Amherst for only two years (despite the identical surname, he was apparently not related to the chief justice). As the trial unfolded, his inexperience became obvious. From Hussey, he elicited the comment that Doyle had a reputation as "a drinking man." Winsby told the defence lawyer that, during his brief visit the day before his death, Clem had remarked that "Doyle was not faithful and he did not like him." Both statements bolstered the prosecution's case.

Samuel Patterson, a surgeon in Pugwash, had performed the autopsy. Clem had died from a gaping wound to one temple that had penetrated two inches into the brain, he revealed. Clem's head and shoulders were peppered with a number of other axe wounds, none of them fatal.

Gray then turned to proving that Doyle had inflicted the wounds. His key witness was John Sentorius, who lived about two miles from Clem and made his living ferrying people across River Philip. He described Doyle as "addicted to liquor" and recalled talking with the defendant on June 27. Doyle had worked for Clem about three months but said he had just been fired. Doyle borrowed a boat and disappeared for about four hours. He returned the boat around midnight and asked to be rowed to the other shore. After Doyle changed his shirt, Sentorius complied.

As they neared the spot where the road to Amherst met the river, Doyle made a strange request. If anyone inquired about his movements, he implored Sentorius, tell them he had headed in the opposite direction. Sentorius was naturally suspicious, but Doyle explained he owed money and "he was going away because he could not pay it." He claimed he had "deluded" a young woman and thought it best he move on. "After a pause," Sentorius told the court, "he then said: 'all my dependence lies in you not telling which way I go.'" With that, Doyle hopped out of the boat and disappeared into the darkness. Later, when he heard about Clem's murder, Sentorius checked the shirt Doyle had discarded in his kitchen. There was a speck of blood on each sleeve.

Halliburton, the defence lawyer, could do little to lessen the impact of the damning evidence. Under cross-examination, Sentorius acknowledged that Doyle "did not appear worried" upon his return with the borrowed boat, "nor in a great hurry."

Another piece of the puzzle came from John Mulroy, whose farm was directly across the river from Clem's cabin. Doyle had dropped in about ten o'clock on the night of June 27, and he was full of questions. The queries seemed "quite natural" at the time, Mulroy said, but in retrospect they took on a sinister air. What time had Clem returned to his farm? Were Pipes's children there, or had they gone to their own home? Clem had returned about six, Doyle was told, and one of his housekeeper's daughters was staying the night. Doyle had no other business with the Mulroys and left within half an hour.

The next person to see Doyle after Sentorius dropped him on the riverbank was George Glendenning. It was about dawn on June 28, and Doyle was walking on the main road about seven miles outside Amherst. He had said his name was Hales, and he had given Glendenning five shillings for a ride into town in his wagon and five more to take him across an expanse of salt marshes to Sackville, a village just over the border in New Brunswick. As the wagon rattled over the dirt roads, Hales had become talkative, saying he had run away from a ship docked at Pugwash. He was heading to Saint John to see his brother, who was also a sailor. Once they reached Sackville, the man had offered more money for a ride to the next village, but Glendenning declined. Asked to identify this fellow Hales, Glendenning pointed across the courtroom to Doyle.

Avard and Filmore recounted their pursuit and capture of Doyle. Besides the wallet containing a large sum of money, their search of Doyle's pockets had turned up two documents. The prosecutor, Gray, called Pugwash merchant Henry Pineo to the witness stand to explain their significance. Doyle had owed money to Pineo and one of the documents showed that Clem had paid off the debt when he hired Doyle to work on his farm. The other document, however, should not have been in the defendant's possession – it recorded a year-old transaction between Pineo and Clem that had nothing to do with Doyle.

Gray zeroed in on the wallet. Abraham Seaman told the court he had repaired a wallet for Clem about eight years earlier, using a black strap because he had no red leather to match. Shown the wallet taken from Doyle, Seaman immediately recognized his handiwork.

Elizabeth Pipes, the housekeeper attacked and left for dead, testified that Clem had gone to Pugwash with Doyle on June 27, then had returned alone about six in the evening. Clem carried his money and papers in a wallet, which he stored in a wooden chest at the head of his bed. A few days before his death, she said, it had contained £40 in banknotes.

"That's the book," she exclaimed when Gray showed her the wallet, "there's no mistake about it."

Halliburton blundered again when it was his turn to question Pipes. She agreed with the defence lawyer's suggestion that Doyle was not a malicious man. Then she dropped a bombshell, recalling an instance when Doyle had threatened to "cut my damned head off when he would catch me alone."

* * *

Given Halliburton's track record with the prosecution's witnesses, it was probably best that he chose to call none for the defence. Doyle had no right to testify. Allowing defendants to give evidence in a criminal trial was forbidden until almost the turn of the century in Canada – it was assumed they would lie to save themselves, especially in murder cases. Doyle did have the right to make a statement to the jury, and he disputed Pipes's testimony. "She never saw that pocketbook before it was taken from me," he insisted. "It belongs to me."

Chief Justice Halliburton was convinced that Doyle was guilty. "It is my duty to tell you that these circumstances weigh most strongly against the prisoner," he said in his instructions to the jury. "The night before the murder the property" – the wallet – "is in Clem's house, and 10 o'clock the same night the prisoner is within half a mile of the house. On Friday morning he is 120 miles off, with the property on him. In the name of God how got he the property? If he is not the person who committed the deed, how came he by the property?"

The jurors filed out to deliberate. They were back within twenty minutes with their verdict: guilty of murder.

"The prisoner, who appeared to have entertained hopes of acquittal to the last, sunk on hearing the verdict. He buried his face in his hands," one journalist wrote of Doyle's reaction. "It was a melancholy spectacle," agreed another, "and it strengthened one in the opinion that the prisoner had entertained the belief that he could not be convicted of the homicide upon circumstantial testimony and presumption."

Doyle continued to sob as the judge sentenced him to die on the gallows in two days. "Never, in the course of a long professional life, have I met with an instance of depravity equal to that with which you now stand convicted," the chief justice intoned. "To the surrounding multitude – let the fate of this unhappy man be a lesson." Doyle's temptation had been "to possess himself solely of the property of another, and that very property which formed the temptation has been the chief means of his detection."

The trial and execution of Doyle, *The Novascotian* editorialized, "afforded a striking exemplification of the strength which circumstantial evidence occasionally assumes." Doyle had the motive and opportunity to commit murder. A red wallet with the black strap, a damning piece of evidence he could have easily tossed by the wayside, had sealed his fate.

Acknowledgments

I have been fascinated by Nova Scotia's rich legal history since the 1980s, when I covered the court beat as a reporter for Halifax's *Daily News* and *Chronicle Herald*. I'm grateful to my former *Herald* editors Jane Purves, Bill March, Lorna Inness, and Clair McIlveen, who encouraged my efforts to tell these stories. A former *Herald* colleague, Bruce Erskine, proofread some of these chapters and Patrick Duncan, now a judge, was generous with insights into the criminal law and the justice system. Staff of the Nova Scotia Archives, the Maritime Museum of the Atlantic, the Legislative Library, the McCord Museum, Library and Archives Canada, the Glace Bay Heritage Museum, and *The Chronicle Herald*'s library patiently fielded my requests for access to records and images. Special thanks to Lesley Choyce of Pottersfield Press, who first published these stories almost three decades ago in two books, *Crime Wave* and *Bluenose Justice*, and welcomed the idea of collecting the best ones in a single volume. Thanks as well to Peggy Amirault and Julia Swan, who edited the manuscript. Most of all, I'm grateful to Kerry Oliver for her support for everything I do.

Sources

The journalists who were feeding the early printing presses learned what all journalists have learned; that crime news is prime news.
                                    – Mitchell Stephens, A History of News

A small army of Nova Scotia's earliest, crime-obsessed journal-ists filed the reports that form the foundation for these stories. The newspapers of an earlier age spared no ink or paper when it came to coverage of crimes and trials, often providing verbatim transcripts of testimony and legal arguments. These accounts are the only surviving record of some trials and many key events.

Some of these reports were sensationalized. Rumours were printed, lending them the veneer of fact. Nineteenth-century news-papers were openly partisan, proudly proclaiming their biases and political beliefs. And too many journalists assumed suspects were guilty long before a court passed judgment. But the sheer number of newspapers that once covered Nova Scotia's courts (as many as a half-dozen were published in Halifax in the mid-1800s) helped to ensure accuracy. Journalists were quick to correct mistakes made by their rivals, leading their readers – and today's researchers – closer to the truth.

To verify press reports and dig deeper into each story, I consulted an array of books and primary sources. The original court files have survived for some of these cases, while research at Nova Scotia's provincial archives turned up case-related letters, reports, petitions, and other documents. The Nova Scotia Supreme Court's official case reports, available online, include rulings on Nicholas Martin's prosecution for murder, the *Zero* mutiny, and the brazen robbers who looted a Halifax bank while the tellers were outside, watching a circus parade. The additional historical accounts, biographies, memoirs, and other published sources listed below allowed me to flesh out the legal, political, and social context of these cases, and provided the detail needed to bring characters and events to life.

Akins, T.B. "History of Halifax City," *Nova Scotia Historical Society Collections*, vol. 8 (1892-94), 3-320.

Bank of Nova Scotia v. Forman et al, in *Nova Scotia Reports*, 1872-75, vol. 3, 141-61.

Beck, J. Murray. "'A Fool for a Client': The Trial of Joseph Howe," *Acadiensis: Journal of the History of the Atlantic Region*, vol. 3 no. 2 (Spring 1974), 27-44.

-------- *The Government of Nova Scotia*. Toronto, ON: University of Toronto Press, 1957.

-------- *Joseph Howe: Volume I, Conservative Reformer, 1804-1848*. Montreal, QC: McGill-Queen's University Press, 1984.

-------- "The Nova Scotian 'Disputed Election' of 1859 and Its Aftermath," *Canadian Historical Review*, vol. 36 (1955), 293-315.

-------- *Politics of Nova Scotia, Volume One: Nicholson-Fielding, 1710-1896*. Glen Margaret, NS: Four East Publications, 1985.

-------- "Rise and Fall of Nova Scotia's Attorney General, 1749-1983," in Peter B. Waite, Sandra Oxner, and Thomas Garden Barnes, eds., *Law in a Colonial Society: The Nova Scotia Experience*. Toronto, ON: Carswell, 1984, 125-42.

Bird, Michael J. *The Town that Died: The True Story of the Greatest Man-made Explosion Before Hiroshima.* New York: Putnam 1963.

Blakeley, Phyllis R. *Glimpses of Halifax, 1867-1900.* Halifax, NS: Public Archives of Nova Scotia, 1949.

Cahill, Barry. "'Fide et fortitudine vivo': The Career of Chief Justice Brian Finucane," *Nova Scotia Historical Society Collections,* vol. 42 (1986), 153-69.

-------- and Jim Phillips. "The Supreme Court of Nova Scotia: Origins to Confederation," in Philip Girard, Jim Phillips, and Barry Cahill, eds., *The Supreme Court of Nova Scotia 1754-2004: From Imperial Bastion to Provincial Oracle.* Toronto, ON: University of Toronto Press, 2004.

Calnek, W.A. *History of the County of Annapolis.* Toronto, ON: William Briggs, 1897, 293-94.

Cameron, Silver Donald. *Schooner: Bluenose and Bluenose II.* Toronto, ON: McClelland and Stewart, 1984.

Chisholm, Joseph A. "Sir Thomas Strange, C.J.," *Canadian Bar Review,* vol. 24 (1946), 600-03.

-------- "The King v. Joseph Howe: Prosecution for Libel," *Canadian Bar Review,* vol. 13 no. 8 (1935), 584-93.

-------- ed. *The Speeches and Public Letters of Joseph Howe, vol. 1* Halifax, NS: Chronicle Publishing Co., 1909.

-------- "Three Chief Justices of Nova Scotia," *Nova Scotia Historical Society Collections,* vol. 28 (1949), 148-58.

Cuthbertson, Brian. *The Old Attorney General: A Biography of Richard John Uniacke.* Halifax, NS: Nimbus Publishing, 1980.

Dennis, Agnes. "Reminiscences of a Halifax Centenarian (Mrs. P.H. Lenoir)," *Nova Scotia Historical Society Collections,* vol. 23 (1936), 2-3.

DesBrisay, Mather B. *History of the County of Lunenburg.* Toronto, ON: William Briggs, 1895, 501-58.

Dictionary of Canadian Biography. Available online: www. biographi.ca.

Doull, John. "Four Attorney-Generals," *Nova Scotia Historical Society Collections,* vol. 27 (1947), 1-16.

-------- "The First Five Attorney-Generals of Nova Scotia," *Nova Scotia Historical Society Collections,* vol. 26 (1945), 33-48.

-------- "Sketches of Attorney Generals of Nova Scotia, 1750-1926" (Unpublished typescript, 1964).

Dubinsky, J. Louis. *In and Out of Court.* Hantsport, NS: Lancelot Press, 1981.

Elliott, Shirley B. *The Legislative Assembly of Nova Scotia, 1758-1983: A Biographical Directory.* Halifax, NS: Province of Nova Scotia, 1984.

Gillespie, G.J. *Bluenose Skipper.* Fredericton, NB: Brunswick Press, 1955.

Greco, Clara. "The Superior Court Judiciary of Nova Scotia, 1754-1900: A Collective Biography," in Philip Girard and Jim Phillips, eds., *Essays in the History of Canadian Law, Volume III: Nova Scotia.* Toronto, ON: University of Toronto Press, 1990, 42-79.

Hale, C.A. *The Early Court Houses of Nova Scotia, vols. 1 and 2,* Manuscript Report No. 293. Ottawa, ON: Parks Canada, 1977.

-------- "Early Court Houses of the Maritime Provinces," in Margaret Carter, comp., *Early Canadian Court Houses.* Ottawa, ON: Parks Canada, 1983, 37-77.

Harris, R.V., comp. *Catalogue of the Portraits of the Judges of the Supreme Court of Nova Scotia and Other Portraits.* Halifax, NS: Law Courts, 1929.

History of the Bank of Nova Scotia, 1832-1900. Halifax, NS: Bank of Nova Scotia, 1901.

Judicial Proceedings Relating to the Murder of Capt. Benson on Board the Brig Zero. Halifax, NS, 1866.

Kesterton, Wilfred H. *A History of Journalism in Canada.* Toronto, ON: McClelland and Stewart, 1967, 21-3.

-------- *The Law and the Press in Canada.* Ottawa, ON: Carleton University Press 1984, 3.

Kimball, R.E. *The Bench: The History of Nova Scotia's Provincial Courts.* Halifax, NS: Province of Nova Scotia, 1989.

Kitz, Janet F. *Shattered City: The Halifax Explosion and the Road to Recovery.* Halifax, NS: Nimbus Publishing, 1989.

Lynch, Charles. *You Can't Print THAT!: Memoirs of a Political Voyeur.* Edmonton, AB: Hurtig, 1983.

Lynch, Peter. "Early Reminiscences of Halifax – Men Who Have Passed From Us," *Nova Scotia Historical Society Collections,* vol. 16 (1912), 171-204.

MacDonald, Peter V. *Court Jesters: Canada's Lawyers and Judges Take the Stand to Relate Their Funniest Stories.* Agincourt, ON: Methuen, 1985.

MacMechan, Archibald. "The *Saladin* Pirates," in *Old Province Tales.* Toronto, ON: McClelland & Stewart, 1924, 207-38.

MacNutt, W.S. *The Atlantic Provinces: The Emergence of Colonial Society.* Toronto, ON: McClelland & Stewart, 1965.

Oxner, Sandra E. "The Evolution of the Lower Court of Nova Scotia," in Peter Waite, Sandra Oxner, and Thomas Garden Barnes, eds., *Law in a Colonial Society: The Nova Scotia Experience.* Toronto, ON: Carswell, 1984, 59-79.

The Queen v. Dowcey, Douglas et al, in *Nova Scotia Reports, 1865-67,* vol. 2 part 1, 93-140.

The Queen v. Nicholas H. Martin, in *Nova Scotia Reports, 1853-55*, vol. 1, 322-26.

The Queen v. Watson et al, in *Nova Scotia Reports, 1876-77*, vol. 2, 1-5.

Raddall, Thomas H. *Halifax: Warden of the North*, rev. ed. Toronto, ON: McClelland & Stewart, 1971.

Russell, Benjamin. *Autobiography of Benjamin Russell*. Halifax, NS: Royal Print & Litho, 1932.

-------- "Reminiscences of the Nova Scotia Judiciary," *Dalhousie Review*, vol. 5 (1925), 499-512.

Saunders, E.M. *Three Premiers of Nova Scotia: The Hon. J. W. Johnstone, the Hon. Joseph Howe, the Hon. Charles Tupper, M.D., C.B.* Toronto, ON: William Briggs, 1909.

Schull, Joseph and J. Douglas Gibson. *A History of the Bank of Nova Scotia, 1832-1982*. Toronto, ON: Macmillan of Canada, 1982.

Smith, James F. "Cumberland County Hatchet Murder," *Nova Scotia Historical Quarterly*, vol. 5 (June 1975), 117-29.

South Shore, Seasoned Timbers, Vol. 2: Some Historic Buildings from Nova Scotia's South Shore. Halifax, NS: Heritage Trust of Nova Scotia, 1974.

The Supreme Court of Nova Scotia and Its Judges: 1754-1978. Halifax, NS: Nova Scotia Barristers' Society, 1978.

Townshend, C.J. "Historical account of the Courts of Judicature in Nova Scotia," *Canadian Law Times*, vol. 19 (1899), 25-37, 58-72, 87-98, 142-57.

-------- *History of the Court of Chancery in Nova Scotia*. Toronto, ON: Carswell, 1900.

-------- "History of the Courts of Chancery in Nova Scotia," *Canadian Law Times*, vol. 20, (1900), 14-21, 37-42, 75-80, 105-17.

Townshend, C.J. "Memoir of the life of the Honorable William Blowers Bliss," *Nova Scotia Historical Society Collections*, vol. 17 (1913), 23-45.

Trial of Jones, Hazelton, Anderson and Trevaskiss, Alias Johnston for Piracy and Murder on Board Barque Saladin. Halifax, NS: Petheric Press, 1967.

Trueman, Howard. *The Chignecto Isthmus and Its First Settlers.* Toronto, ON: William Briggs, 1902.

Waite, Peter B. *The Man From Halifax: Sir John Thompson, Prime Minister.* Toronto, ON: University of Toronto Press, 1985.

Willis, John. *A History of Dalhousie Law School.* Toronto, ON: University of Toronto Press, 1979.

About the Author

Dean Jobb is an award-winning Nova Scotia author and journalist who specializes in recreating crimes that offer a window on the past.

His book *Empire of Deception* (published in 2015 by Algonquin Books in the United States and HarperCollins Canada), the story of 1920s Chicago con man Leo Koretz and his escape to a life of luxury and excess in Nova Scotia, won the Chicago Writers Association and Crime Writers of Canada book-of-the-year awards and was a finalist for Canada's top award for nonfiction, the Hilary Weston Writers' Trust Prize.

He is also the author of *The Acadians: A People's Story of Exile and Triumph. Calculated Risk: Greed, Politics and the Westray Disaster*, his groundbreaking investigation of the explosion that killed twenty-six workers at Nova Scotia's Westray coal mine in 1992, was runner-up for Canada's National Business Book Award. In 2021 Algonquin Books and HarperCollins Canada will publish *The Case of the Murderous Dr. Cream: The Hunt for a Victorian Era Serial Killer.*

Dean writes a monthly true crime column, "Stranger Than Fiction," for *Ellery Queen's Mystery Magazine* and is a contributing writer for the *Chicago Review of Books*. His work has appeared in Canadian, American, and European publications. He was a reporter, editor, and political columnist during a twenty-year newspaper career with the Halifax *Chronicle Herald*. His investigative reports have been nominated for Canada's National Newspaper and National Magazine awards and he is a three-time winner of Atlantic Canada's top journalism award.

Dean is a professor in the School of Journalism at the University of King's College in Halifax, where he is an instructor and cohort director in the Master of Fine Arts in Creative Nonfiction Program. He is the author of the textbook *Media Law for Canadian Journalists* and has contributed chapters to books on a range of subjects, including true crime, research and storytelling techniques, press freedom, and the birth of political satire. He lives in Wolfville, Nova Scotia.

Books by Dean Jobb

Empire of Deception:
From Chicago to Nova Scotia – The Incredible Story of a Master Swindler Who Seduced a City and Captivated a Nation

A riveting tale of greed, glamour, and one of the greatest swindles in history – the exploits of 1920s Chicago con man extraordinaire Leo Koretz and his escape to a new life in Nova Scotia. He ran one of the longest, most elaborate, and most successful swindles in history. For almost twenty years the lawyer enticed hundreds of people to invest as much as $30 million (upwards of $400 million today), most of it in phantom timberland and oil wells in Panama. His Bayano River Syndicate, he claimed, controlled millions of acres, including oilfields that produced a torrent of crude and earned investors an astounding sixty percent return. *Empire of Deception* recreates an era when it seemed as if everyone was entitled to easy riches – heady times not so different from our own. The incredible-but-true saga of Leo Koretz and his spectacular Jazz Age swindle exposes the pitfalls, then and now, of too much trust, too much greed, and too little common sense.

Calculated Risk:
Greed, Politics and the Westray Tragedy

Calculated Risk is the only comprehensive account of the worst mine disaster in modern Canadian history – Nova Scotia's 1992 Westray coal mine explosion. On May 8, 1992, twenty-six men went underground to work the night shift at the Westray coal mine in Pictou County, Nova Scotia. They never came back. The massive explosion that claimed their lives the next morning sent shock waves around the world. *Calculated Risk* recounts the stories of the miners who died and the families they left behind, as well as the corporate and political machinations behind the development of the ill-fated mine. The product of two years of research and featuring exclusive interviews with key figures in the tragedy, the book exposes the safety lapses, political intrigues, and business decisions that culminated in disaster.

The Acadians:
A People's Story of Exile and Triumph

This is the story of one of the great crimes of history, a brutal act of ethnic cleansing committed in the 1750s in what is now the Canadian provinces of Nova Scotia, New Brunswick, and Prince Edward Island. The victims were the descendants of the region's French settlers, who called themselves Acadians and their homeland Acadie. Geography and history conspired to trap the Acadians in the crossfire as France and Britain fought for supremacy over North America. More than 10,000 people were removed at gunpoint and sent into exile along the east coast of North America, France, England, and South America. Five thousand, maybe more, died of disease and deprivation or perished in shipwrecks. Families and friends were separated, never to be reunited. An entire generation knew nothing but the squalor of refugee camps and prisons and the uncertainty of a nomadic life.

The deportation was calculated to destroy a people and wipe out a distinct culture, but it failed. Today, there are an estimated three million Acadian descendants worldwide. Acadians who escaped deportation and those who returned established new communities in Atlantic Canada, where they now number close to 300,000. This is a story filled with heroes and villains, as well as ordinary men and women caught up in extraordinary events. This is a story of the triumph of the human spirit in the face of cruelty and unimaginable hardship.